AMERICAN IDOLS

The American Church's Compromise,
and How to Correct Course

DAVID M. JOHNSON

Copyright © 2022 David M. Johnson.

All rights reserved. No part of this book may be used or reproduced by any means, graphic, electronic, or mechanical, including photocopying, recording, taping or by any information storage retrieval system without the written permission of the author except in the case of brief quotations embodied in critical articles and reviews.

This book is a work of non-fiction. Unless otherwise noted, the author and the publisher make no explicit guarantees as to the accuracy of the information contained in this book and in some cases, names of people and places have been altered to protect their privacy.

WestBow Press books may be ordered through booksellers or by contacting:

WestBow Press
A Division of Thomas Nelson & Zondervan
1663 Liberty Drive
Bloomington, IN 47403
www.westbowpress.com
844-714-3454

Because of the dynamic nature of the Internet, any web addresses or links contained in this book may have changed since publication and may no longer be valid. The views expressed in this work are solely those of the author and do not necessarily reflect the views of the publisher, and the publisher hereby disclaims any responsibility for them.

Any people depicted in stock imagery provided by Getty Images are models, and such images are being used for illustrative purposes only. Certain stock imagery © Getty Images.

Scriptures taken from the Holy Bible, New International Version®, NIV®. Copyright © 1973, 1978, 1984, 2011 by Biblica, Inc.™ Used by permission of Zondervan. All rights reserved worldwide. www.zondervan.com The "NIV" and "New International Version" are trademarks registered in the United States Patent and Trademark Office by Biblica, Inc.®

ISBN: 978-1-6642-5201-1 (sc)
ISBN: 978-1-6642-5203-5 (hc)
ISBN: 978-1-6642-5202-8 (e)

Library of Congress Control Number: 2021924831

Print information available on the last page.

WestBow Press rev. date: 06/23/2022

I would like to dedicate this book to my Lord and Savior, Jesus Christ, who turned my life around many years ago and who graciously continues to work in me and on me, conforming me to live as though I am a Christ follower. This is my aim and my goal.

My wife, Lori, has been an incredible support to me over the years and has heard me talk through the concepts in this book for a long time, encouraging me to finally step out and get it published!

I literally could not have done this if it weren't for them.

Those who cling to worthless idols forfeit
the grace that could be theirs.
—Jonah 2:8

The thief comes only to steal, kill, and destroy;
I have come that they might have life, and have it to the full.
—John 10:10

INTRODUCTION

It wasn't a fair fight.
One man, standing alone with a crowd of priests against him.
One man, standing alone with the King of the land against him.
One man, standing alone with a throng of people in the community against him.

Hardly a fair fight!

You've seen situations like that before.
One man stands in China's Tiananmen Square, facing off against a line of tanks.
One woman, tired of the double standard, refuses to "move to the back of the bus."
One man, threatened with death, continues to lead a nation to aspire to "live out the meaning of their creed."

This one man stood alone, against 450 prophets of Baal, a ruthless king Ahab, and a throng of people—the nation of Israel—and demanded that they declare their allegiance. "If the Lord is God, follow Him; if Baal is God, follow him!"
The people stood still, noncommittal.
He was alone.
He challenged the servants of Baal (1 Kings 18).
He stood against them alone—sort of.

Physically, he was alone. In reality, He had the Lord on his side.
So it wasn't a fair fight, but the one who actually had the power was Elijah!
He had the God of the universe on his side. What chance did the 450 prophets and their king stand?

If you know the story, you know that Elijah let the prophets of Baal go first—to call to him and urge him to show himself in power. All day long they called, but to no avail. Elijah taunted, "Maybe he's asleep. Call louder!" However, no one answered.
Then it was Elijah's turn. He prepared the altar, the sacrifice, and the wood. Then he did something unusual. He had everything doused with water three times! The water ran off and filled the trench around the altar.

> "Then Elijah called out, "Lord, the God of Abraham, Isaac and Israel, let it be known today that you are God in Israel and that I am your servant and have done all these things at your command. Answer me, Lord, answer me, so these people will know that you, Lord, are God, and that you are turning their hearts back again."
>
> Then the fire of the Lord fell and burned up the sacrifice, the wood, the stones and the soil, and also licked up the water in the trench."
>
> How did the people react? "The Lord, He is God; the Lord, He is God!" (1 Kings 18:36–39)

Better late than never, I guess!
Idolatry is a word we usually associate with ancient times, primitive peoples, and rituals. It is not a word we usually associate with ourselves

and today's times. After all, we are "postmodern." We are *enlightened*, and we are *evolved*, right?

Many things have changed dramatically since Bible times—especially Old Testament times. (Heck, there are many things that have changed since I was a kid!) Yet the human heart hasn't really changed all that much. The things we love, the things we long for, the things that really "touch" us at our core. We still smile when we see a baby in their mother's arms, we still have hope when we see a bride and groom on their wedding day, and we still shed a tear when we see death intrude in the lives of loved ones.

The human heart has also remained consistent in its fickle nature. We are wishy-washy when it comes to commitment. We have an uncanny ability to forget the "important" things in life. Many of the things that seemed to be important to us yesterday are seemingly forgotten today. Even some of our most important relationships we have in life—the ones that we are excited about, committed to, and passionately pursuing—can lose their momentum and stall if we're not careful. The people you went to bed dreaming about last night can become yesterday's news if you're not careful.

The human heart is consistent in its inconsistent nature.
The scriptures say that we should "guard your hearts, for it is the wellspring of life" (Proverbs 4:23).

The wellspring—the source.

When you picture a flowing river or drinking from a clear mountain spring, the "wellspring" is the source of that water. What the writer of the book of Proverbs is saying here is that we need to protect our hearts, because out of it flows everything! Our dreams, our hopes, our priorities, our loves, our values—they all flow from the heart.

Jesus knew the importance of the heart.

Once He was being challenged and was asked why He allowed His disciples to eat without first washing their hands in the *officially sanctioned* way. He replied,

> "The things that come out of the mouth come from the heart, and these make a man "unclean." For out of the heart come evil thoughts, murder, adultery, sexual immorality, theft, false testimony, slander. These are what make a man "unclean," but eating with unwashed hands does not make him "unclean." (Matthew 15:18–20)

He challenged them to get their eyes off the external, superficial things. Why were they getting worked up about the state of their hands when they eat? Instead, they should focus on the real stuff! Focus on the source of "uncleanness"; focus on the heart!

Later, Jesus was being challenged on His understanding of the Law and the prophets (essentially the Old Testament). He was asked, 'OK, you're so smart. What's the greatest commandment?'

Jesus replied,

> "Love the Lord your God with all your heart and with all your soul and with all your mind." This is the first and greatest commandment. And the second is like it: "Love your neighbor as yourself." All the Law and the Prophets hang on these two commandments." (Matthew 22:36–38)

Jesus knew it is in the heart—in the core of our souls—where we determine what we're about. That's where we set our values and priorities. That's where we determine what we love and what defines us.

One problem: the human heart is easily deceived and very often self-centered.

Jeremiah 17:9 says, "The heart is deceitful above all things and wicked beyond cure. Who can know it?"

It's one of the things that unites humanity—across miles, continents, and time zones. Across decades, centuries, and millennia even!

The human heart can be easily deceived and can be selfish to the extreme.

Think about it: What child had to be taught to be selfish? Have parents ever had to teach their kids to demand their own way? Have we ever had to teach them to think of themselves first?

No! Every child has this nature within themselves and will resort to it if allowed. In other words, every child—every person—has selfish impulses within.

Unless some other source comes on us to change that situation, we will exhibit the thoughts and behaviors that make us (from God's perspective) "unclean" (to use Jesus's word).

So what's this have to do with "idolatry"? Simply this: if we are not careful, and if we don't have the spiritual input necessary to change our hearts, we will be *prone* to idolatry.

How does that show itself?

An excellent question, and one I hope to help answer in this book.

The truth is, as John Calvin said, "Man's nature, so to speak, is a perpetual factory of idols."[1]

If we understand the Lord's character—His loving, wise, holy, gracious, and good character—we will begin to understand that *He* deserves our trust more than *we* do—and certainly more than our culture does!

If we start to trust Him, knowing that His teachings come from His love for us, we will then begin to understand that the decision to conform our will to His is a wise one. As the apostle Paul wrote,

---

[1] Calvin's *Institutes*, chapter 11.

> "Do not be conformed to the pattern of this world, but be transformed by the renewing of your mind. Then you will be able to test and approve what God's will is—His good, pleasing, and perfect will!" (Romans 12:1–2)

As we learn to trust His will and follow it, we will find that it is for our good!

I invite you to come along and consider the many ways we—especially in America—have made, and even worshipped, idols and how we can correct ourselves! I can almost guarantee you that some of the things I write will bother you. Some may even offend you. I don't take that lightly. Believe me!

However, I firmly believe, and I believe that the scriptures teach, that we when we are forced to confront ways that we have not lived according to His Word, and when we come to see beliefs and opinions that we've held that do not line up with His Word, then the best thing we can do—the *only* real option for Christ followers—is to repent and correct our thinking. This leads to the possibility of experiencing the reality of His "good, pleasing, and perfect will" (Romans 12:2).

CHAPTER 1
PRACTICAL IDOLATRY

I RECENTLY WENT ON VACATION WITH MY FAMILY.

When we go on vacation, it is often camping, and this time was no exception. We camped in one of our favorite Michigan parks, Van Buren State Park, on the shores of Lake Michigan.

We love the sounds, the smells, and the feel of camping. We love the sunsets and campfires. We *love* the s'mores!

I don't know about you, but when I go on vacation, I like to relax. That may sound obvious, but some of our vacations have been so busy—so filled with *vacation activities*—that we've ended up more stressed and fatigued after it than we were going into it!

Not this time. This time, we were deliberately spending a lot more time just 'chillin'.

Even with that being the case, I like to get up early. I like to rise before anyone else and have my cup of coffee, watch the campground wake up, read the Word of God, pray, and generally ease into my day.

On this vacation, however, I did things differently. On at least two mornings, I had my alarm set for 6:30 and was motivated to get up and start the coffee and so on.

But on a couple of these mornings, the temperature was just perfect: cool but not cold. The campground was quiet, the birds were singing, and it felt unusually good to continue lying there in bed. I figured I could just lie there for a few more minutes and then get up. I silenced my alarm quickly and continued lying there 'just for a few minutes.'

Well, you can see where this is going. About an hour later, I awoke. It was much lighter, more of the campground was up and going, and I didn't have much time to ease into my day.

As it turned out, my family must've been more tired than I was because they kept right on sleeping!

Now it's true that on vacation, this doesn't really matter. But what if that happened on a Sunday morning? As a Pastor, this is one of those recurring nightmares that I have: I oversleep and end up delivering my sermon in my pajamas with morning breath!

Or what if it happened on the day you had that big medical test?

Or the morning of your interview for your dream job?

In those cases, silencing your alarm could be harmful.

In most cases, alarm bells can be very helpful, but only if you listen to them.

I believe there are alarm bells ringing in our world—and in America in particular—that many Americans are not listening to.

We have simply hit snooze.

Worse yet, many of us have stopped wanting to hear the alarms.

I believe, in fact, that alarm bells are ringing within the church! Are we listening to them, or have we grown so accustomed to them that we don't hear them anymore?

Even worse, have we now begun to resent those who sound the alarms?

Let me be blunt: I believe that our country, and our churches, are in potentially serious condition *because* we're ignoring the alarm bells! What do I mean?

I think there are some areas of great concern in our nation right now, and I want to tell you this because I believe there's *hope*—and a good future—but *only* for those who heed the alarms!

The first is our political climate.

Political corruption is rampant in our nation's capital and even in our state capitals—on *both* sides of the aisle. Politicians, lobbyists, and organizations are working to change the very core of America.

That which we once stood for—liberty, freedom, and opportunity—are increasingly being relegated to past history or even (in some minds) archaic values that need to be reinterpreted and even revolutionized.

There are some who want to fundamentally transform America—not for the good and not to take the "self-evident truths" of the past (all men are created equal, they are endowed by their Creator with certain inalienable rights, that among these are life, liberty, and the pursuit of happiness) but in a new, less Creator-inspired, and more self-centered way. Others want to "make America great again," as if it was God's nation on earth and we have always been His people.

One problem is that the political climate is so divisive in this country that it becomes very difficult for people to have productive discussions on these issues and to come to any reasonable conclusion.

Our last three election cycles have been increasingly hostile and divisive. The political climate has both reflected and affected our social climate. Family members and friends who used to agree to disagree are now attacking each other, with claims of racism and communism. President Obama famously said to Republican leaders just after his 2008 election win, "Elections have consequences." And President Trump would say…whatever he wanted! The diplomacy of former leaders seems to be gone. Now President Biden has come in purporting to be a "uniter"; however, the political wrangling has not changed.

The Covid 19 virus has hit us hard, and after a couple of months of giving the benefit of the doubt, we have started to make accusations to come up with conspiracy theories about the other side, and so on.

And the alarm bells keep ringing.

The second area of concern is our economy.

Our country, and much of the world, is in danger of economic meltdown. Our economies are so interwoven now that if one country's economy falters—as many are doing—the others who are less bad off are forced to step in and bail them out. The problem is that puts those formerly healthy countries at greater risk. If an economic storm then rises, more countries—including the United States—become endangered.

When we add to that the fact very few politicians on either side of the aisle seem to want to break that news to the American people—and that (increasingly) *the American people don't want to hear it*, no matter how true it is—we have a potential disaster on our hands.

Enter COVID-19. It has taken a strong, vibrant economy and tanked it. Millions are unemployed, businesses are failing, and the governments of the world are simply fabricating money in order to keep the people somewhat solvent financially. Now record levels of inflation have hit every area of our economy, and families are facing serious financial difficulty.

Question: If we had another Great Depression today, do you think the American people would react the same way they did back in the 1920s—by helping each other out, pooling resources, and supporting one another? I don't, because I don't think the American people are anywhere near the same as they were back then.

And the alarm bells keep ringing.

This leads to my third big area of concern: our collective morality. The moral fabric of our society has changed.

Today, Americans are much more likely to take to the streets and riot, demanding that someone else pay for bailouts and provide for their needs. At the same time, they are *less* likely to form communities where people share with each other and help each other out, not waiting for some rich guy or the big government to step in and save the day.

Our collective consciousness of what it means to be an American is very different today from in times past.

As a culture, our country tends to be much more self-centered and much more willing to blame someone else than to take personal responsibility for ourselves, our families, and our communities.

An example is abortion.

Since 1973, the US Supreme Court has cited a constitutional right to privacy, which extended to women and the babies they carried. This right said that women have the right to do what they wanted with their own bodies, even to the point of killing a child they are carrying during pregnancy, and that the state could not stand in the way of that right. Since that time, over 62 *million* abortions have been performed in this country. Currently, abortions are performed in all three trimesters of pregnancy, for any and all reasons.

Anyone who says they want to curtail any portion of this practice is immediately branded as a right-wing ideologue and written off as anti-woman. Currently, late-term abortions are common, long past the medical viability stage. In fact, some practitioners and hospitals have even gone so far as to develop policies against intervention and lifesaving, if the baby is mistakenly born alive! Staff are, in some cases, directed to let the baby die.[2]

Recently, the state of New York passed a law to allow abortion for the entire term of pregnancy—with no restrictions—with the effect that a baby one day from due date could be aborted, as long as

---

[2] BBC, June 5, 2018, "The Failed Abortion Survivor Whose Mum Thought She Was Dead."

the health of the mother was deemed at risk.[3] Those terms were not defined. In response to the passage of that law, New York Governor Andrew Cuomo ordered that One World Trade Center—the landmark building that replaced the World Trade Center's Twin Towers—be lit up in pink to celebrate. There were applause and cheers in the governor's office that day.

In Washington, DC, a bill was introduced to protect babies that were mistakenly born alive after a failed abortion. That bill failed to pass.

The fabric of our nation has changed.

Recently, our politicians have bowed to pressure, and our courts have found that marriage—a God-designed institution and a building block of any healthy society—can be redefined. Rather than defining it as people from the dawn of civilization have—as one man and one woman in a monogamous relationship of commitment—we have decided that we can change it simply because of pressure from a small group of people. We have now legalized same-sex marriage in most states, and anyone who tries to speak against it or who refuses to take part in it is branded as homophobic and very often run out of business. Or worse!

And the alarm bells keep ringing.

This leads to the most important area of concern for me: the Church in America has lost its voice and its role as an influencer in our culture.

There are many reasons for this.

Some churches have for decades adopted a mindset of separation from the culture so much that they have become irrelevant to the culture at large, hurling insults and judgments occasionally but impacting it less and less and communicating God's Word, along with His love and concern, less and less.

---

[3] *Washington Examiner,* March 25, 2021, "Disgusting: New York Not Only Legalized Late-Term Abortions, but Also Celebrated Like It Won the Super Bowl."

Other churches have in recent decades sought to be *so* relevant within our culture that they've lost the willingness, ability, or even the sensitivity to God's standards such that they've been assimilated into the culture instead of changing the culture for good—according to God's standards.

Within those churches exist individual Christians who are so concerned about being thought of as "tolerant" and "enlightened" in their thinking and standards that they've completely lost any hope of actually changing their little corner of society.

Some individual Christians have lost touch with God and His heart so much that they would actually be offended if challenged to live lives that point people to Jesus Christ. After all, they'd protest, this would make them seem narrow-minded or judgmental.

They've forgotten that the most loving thing you can do for someone who's lost is to help them find their way. And make no mistake about it: from God's perspective, millions of Americans are "lost" *eternally!* Americans have access to "the Way" (Jesus Christ), yet increasing numbers are not sharing Him.

Jesus calls us to be "salt" and "light" in this world, but many of us have simply opted out.

> Jesus said "God blesses you when people mock you and persecute you and lie about you and say all sorts of evil things against you because you are my followers. Be happy about it! Be very glad! For a great reward awaits you in heaven. And remember, the ancient prophets were persecuted in the same way.
>
> "You are the salt of the earth. But what good is salt if it has lost its flavor? Can you make it salty again? It will be thrown out and trampled underfoot as worthless.

"You are the light of the world—like a city on a hilltop that cannot be hidden. No one lights a lamp and then puts it under a basket. Instead, a lamp is placed on a stand, where it gives light to everyone in the house. In the same way, let your good deeds shine out for all to see, so that everyone will praise your heavenly Father." (Matthew 5:11–16)

If we Christians are ever going to be what Jesus said we were—salt and light—in this world again, we must *first* grapple with the fact that each one of us may be so influenced by our world culture right now that we've (in Jesus's words) *lost our saltiness.*

We may need to own up to the fact that we—individually—have compromised our faith principles.

Maybe we've been so intent on "fitting in" that we've forgotten that God wants us to "stand out."

Perhaps we've bought into some of the philosophy of this world and compromised our belief in God's Word as *the* standard.

Maybe we've just lost touch with our Savior, grown *cold* or *crusty* in our relationship with Him, and need a personal spiritual revival.

It is possible—in fact, I think it's probable—that some in the church members have been lulled to sleep and been deceived into spiritual idolatry.

That's right: *idolatry. Not* in the sense of bowing down to a statue but in another sense.

Here is my working definition of *idolatry:* worship, service, or devotion to something that is not God, as though it were God; giving God's rightful place of ultimate devotion to someone or something else.

The alarm bells are ringing.

Our culture desperately needs the church to get this right!

Our culture needs Christians who are willing to stand up, say, "I love you" and "I will do whatever I can to help you," but who also say, "I'm going to point you to Jesus Christ; ultimately, you need Him!"

If we are *not* willing to do that—because of a mindset, priority, or value that we've adopted that is not centered on Him—then we are guilty of spiritual idolatry.

We can learn a lot about idolatry today from looking at it back in the Bible.

Starting with the Old Testament, we can learn from the people.

The people of Israel had a unique national relationship to God, but we in the church also have a unique relationship. And if we let things of this world come between us and God, if we allow values of this world take over our passions and devotion, *we* are guilty of idolatry just like they were.

Remember that when God selected Abram to become the "father" of a people—the nation of Israel—and decided to work to reveal His will on earth through them, they were surrounded by nations that did not know Him or worship Him. In fact, many of these nations did things God found "detestable." That's part of the reason—after He had taken them out of Egypt—that He said this:

> "I am the Lord your God, who rescued you from the land of Egypt, the place of your slavery. You must not have any other god but me." (Exodus 20:1–3)

God made it very clear that *He* was (and is) the One True God; all those nations around them were following false gods, and their practices—especially their worship of those gods—was detestable to Him.

Israel was to worship and follow Him very differently—and not to compromise at all with the cultures around them.

> "Hear, O Israel: The LORD our God, the LORD is one. Love the LORD your God with all your heart and with all your soul and with all your strength." (Deuteronomy 6:4–5)

Again, at one point, after the people of Israel had heard from Moses and were renewing their commitment to God under the leadership of Joshua, the Word of the Lord came to them like this:

> "Today I have given you the choice between life and death, between blessings and curses. Now I call on heaven and earth to witness the choice you make. Oh, that you would choose life, so that you and your descendants might live!
>
> You can make this choice by loving the LORD your God, obeying him, and committing yourself firmly to him. This is the key to your life. And if you love and obey the LORD, you will live long in the land the LORD swore to give your ancestors Abraham, Isaac, and Jacob." (Deuteronomy 30:19–20)

The point is that God *wanted* to bless the people of Israel and that the *best* way to do this is by their consistent following of His Law! He lays it out *for their good!*

And the alarm bells kept ringing.

There is a persistent pattern we see throughout the scriptures. God—through direct interaction (Abraham, Moses, Joshua) or the prophets (Elijah, Isaiah, Jeremiah, etc.)—communicates to the people when they are in danger of idolatry. The process goes like this:

- God reminds them of His blessings
- warning of trouble ahead
- call to repentance (if heeded, mercy, and if not, restoration)
- discipline
- repentance
- possible restoration

Despite many warnings, the people of Israel showed dramatically bad memory. They continually dropped their guard. They intermarried with those who did not share that special relationship with God, and they began to compromise.

Not only did they fail to worship, honor, follow, and love the Lord their God, but they actually began adopting some of the standards and practices of the nations around them.

And the alarm bells kept ringing.

The people of Israel began to compromise with the nations around them morally, even intermarrying, although forbidden by God. Even more seriously, they began to worship the 'gods' of the nations around them.

Ahab compromised God's standards by marrying a woman named Jezebel from the nations around them. She was a princess in the land of the Phoenicians.

Jezebel brought Baal worship into Israel in a big way.

Baal worship

- involved sexual promiscuity, orgies, and sex of all kinds
- involved child sacrifice
- involved nature worship (worship/sacrifice to the gods of nature)
- was an atmosphere of revelry and debauchery.

Jezebel brought in 450 prophets of Baal to join four hundred prophets of Asherah, all of whom apparently "ate at Jezebel's table" (1 Kings 18:19).

Jezebel killed prophets of the Lord (1 Kings 18:4; 19:10). But God was not intimidated!

God called His prophet, Elijah, to stand up to the prophets of Baal (begins in 1 Kings 18).

Not much is known about Elijah, but he came out of nowhere and pronounced God's judgment on Ahab, Jezebel, and the nation. There would now be a drought—not one drop of rain—until he said otherwise (at God's leading).

Three years went by, but rather than repent and seek the Lord, these people persecuted prophets of God, targeted Elijah as *public enemy number one*, and worshipped and served Baal even more.

Elijah called Ahab to bring the people and all the prophets of Baal to Mount Carmel.

There would be a showdown.

When all the people were assembled, he called out,

> How much longer will you waver, hobbling between two opinions? If the Lord is God, follow him! But if Baal is God, then follow him!" But the people were completely silent. (1 Kings 18:21)

Elijah did not back down from confrontation. He knew who the *true* God was and who was false. He set up a confrontation to *demand* that the people choose.

And God showed up!

> Immediately the fire of the Lord flashed down from heaven and burned up the young bull, the wood, the

stones, and the dust. It even licked up all the water in the trench!

The response of the people?

And when all the people saw it, they fell face down on the ground and cried out, "The LORD—he is God! Yes, the LORD is God!"

The people were reminded again. Finally, they remembered, as if coming out of a trance.

The Lord is God!

Then Elijah commanded, "Seize all the prophets of Baal. Don't let a single one escape!" So the people seized them all, and Elijah took them down to the Kishon Valley and killed them there. (1 Kings 18:38–40)

There was absolute victory because there is *One* God.
There can be no compromise!

God would not allow them to intermingle and to have it both ways. They had to know that there was a choice to make: declare utter allegiance to God and serve Him only or worship false gods and suffer the consequences.

He is God. He deserved their worship.

He is God. Following Him leads to blessing in this life and the next.

He is God. Following Him, even if it means persecution, is the right thing to do.

So what's this got to do with today?

We have many modern 'idols' that are 'worshipped' in our culture, including the following:

- Materialism. Here and now thinking. Living for more "stuff."
- Sexual immorality.

    Virtually anything goes. Putting limits on any and all expressions of sexuality is no longer allowed. Our culture has recently flown right past "gay marriage" to "transgenderism," the belief that gender is an artificial construct, a man-made idea, and that truly "enlightened" people embrace all fifty-six (according to Facebook) variations on "gender."

- Pantheism and nature worship.

    Beyond caring for creation, this has become an obsession with some, a religion, for all practical purposes, where 'the universe is god.'

- Child sacrifice—practical and physical.

    We allow the abortion of millions of human beings each and every year. Many celebrate that right. To date, approximately 62,503,000 abortions have been legally performed in America since 1973.[4]

    On a practical level, we sacrifice our children's right to real childhood on the altar of convenience, experience, and materialism. We want what we want—and we can't let our kids get in the way.

---

[4] LifeNews.com, 1:18–21.

- Worship of man. The opinions of others; the desire to fit in.
- Moral relativism. Anything *must* be allowed, and there are *no* absolutes (which, of course, is a very 'absolute-ish' statement).
- Religious pluralism. The belief that all roads lead to god and that all religions and belief systems are equal. They are all mixtures of truth and error, and "they all basically say the same thing" (wrong!), so we can't treat any one as true and others as false.

Even, in some ways, worship of self.

What, then, is to be our response?

We can learn a lot from the people of Israel, even if we don't have the opportunity—yet—to see a major confrontation between the one true God and our "idols."

We need our response to be the simple, three-step process they showed, as follows:

1) Repent.
2) Worship the true God.

> They fell face down on the ground and cried out, "The Lord—he is God! Yes, the Lord is God!" (1 Kings 18:39)

3) Live holy lives!

> "And so, dear brothers and sisters, I plead with you to give your bodies to God because of all he has done for you. Let them be a living and holy sacrifice—the kind he will find acceptable. This is truly the way to worship him...

> Don't copy the behavior and customs of this world, but let God transform you into a new person by changing the way you think. Then you will learn to know God's will for you, which is good and pleasing and perfect." (Romans 12:1–2)

God has *good* things in store for us.

He *wants* to bless us—to give "good gifts," and "life to the full." But He will only do so as we repent of our own version of idolatry. As we turn back to Him, we say with our mouths and reaffirm with our lives, "The Lord is God!"

If we are willing to listen for His voice today and heed His call to acknowledge and repent of our "idolatry," then He will show Himself in powerful ways in our lives and will lead us to personal spiritual revival!

And as fellow believers in Jesus Christ commit themselves to this as well, we will see whole churches revived. Through them, whole communities can be impacted!

Who knows? Perhaps God will do a major thing in our culture today and lead America to Himself.

We can be sure that is His desire.

He is calling to us today, "Choose you this day who you will serve; as for me and my family, we will serve the Lord!" (Joshua 24:15).

I invite you to join me as we consider together several of the more influential "American idols" that are operating in our culture and in our church and as we consider what we can do to change this!

CHAPTER 2
THE IDOL OF "SELF'

IN MY HIGH SCHOOL DAYS, I WAS VERY POPULAR. I KNOW THAT sounds conceited, and to be honest, at the time, I was. I didn't always have it that way, but in the ninth through twelfth grades, I was in good standing with many people.

- senior class president (technically a co-president, but I digress)
- most votes on homecoming court (in that day, we didn't have kings and queens of homecoming, because someone thought that would be divisive, but if we did …)
- lots of friends from every group: jocks, stoners, motorheads, brains, girls, guys—even teachers!

My goal of being popular was met.
People thought (for the most part) very highly of me.
I'd pulled it off!

Unfortunately, I'd done so at the cost of my character. I had compromised so much of my character that my life was (secretly) a complete mess!

Drugs, alcohol, smoking, sex, lying, breakups, hiding things from my parents—all of these things and more were what constituted "the choice" I had made. This was how I had worked it out.

I had told myself that that was what needed to be done to reach my goal of popularity.

Faith in God? *Ha!*

I had grown up going to church, and in fact, I can remember having a conversation with a friend in eighth grade that I would never be "stupid enough" to smoke. Yet within a year, everything had changed.

Why?

I believe it's because I had adopted a spiritual idol—probably the one that is most prevalent today in America (and certainly every country everywhere deals with it).

Remember, as I stated in chapter 1, the definition of *idolatry* as we're using it is this: worship, service, or devotion to something that is not God, as though it were God; giving God's rightful place of ultimate devotion to someone or something else.

There is one idol that I think comes before all others in our world: the idol of *self*.

Self has become one of the primary 'gods' of this age!

An overemphasis on self—self-respect, self-image, self-satisfaction—can often lead to *self*-indulgence, *self*ishness, *self*-serving, and *self*-centeredness.

The psychology of our culture is to seek our own satisfaction first, then think about others. This has led to all sorts of moral compromises, for which we feel justified since our goal is 'self-fulfillment.' It has led to various forms of escapism, including everything from drug and alcohol addiction to fixations on shopping, video games, pornography, gambling, etc.

This *self-first* mindset is what leads to us who claim to be followers of Jesus to live as though we're not.

This is one explanation for the spiritual compromise that many of us are guilty of, which shows up everywhere from the kind of TV shows we watch to the ungodlike things we post on social media and the jokes we tell (or at least laugh at) in the office.

It has also affected our relationship with God to the extent that we end up requiring God to fit in to our own agenda. We treat our faith (and the Word of God) as a *cafeteria plan*, picking and choosing as we see fit.

It hasn't always been this way.

Back in the 1950s, a psychologist named Carl Rogers came on the scene. He began a new kind of treatment of people that was called "person-centered therapy."[5] It was somewhat revolutionary in that it taught an emphasis on the 'self' and that the key to fixing problems was how a client looked at himself first and foremost.

A therapist's job was to help the client come to his own solutions.

At the same time, another psychologist, Abraham Maslow, came along and published something called Maslow's Hierarchy of Needs.[6] Maslow's theory was that every person has levels of 'need,' and these needs are driving us—even though we are unaware.

At the base are our "Physiological Needs": breathing, food, water, sex, sleep, etc.

Just above that on Maslow's hierarchy is the level of "Safety Needs": security of body, employment, resources, morality, family, health, property, and so on.

---

[5] https://en.wikipedia.org/wiki/Person-centered_therapy.
[6] https://en.wikipedia.org/wiki/Maslow%27s_hierarchy_of_needs.

The next level of need is the "Love and Belonging Needs," where we need family, friendship, and sexual intimacy.

Just above that is our "Esteem Needs" level, where we focus on self-esteem, confidence, achievement, respect of others, and being respected by others.

The highest level in Maslow's hierarchy is "Self-Actualization Needs." This is where we can focus on morality, creativity, spirituality, problem-solving, and others.

The theory behind these levels is that it is difficult, if not impossible, to focus on the higher levels of needs until we have successfully met the lower levels of needs.

Why do I tell you all this?

Because it was around that time—the mid to late fifties—that the "self" became a driving value in our culture. This led in many ways to the drug and so-called "free love" culture of the sixties, and so on.

It has not stopped.

Back in the 1970s, *SELF* magazine[7] was founded. It had a subscription of about 1.5 million people, and its focus was, essentially, how to become the best "self" you can be. *SELF* became a digital-only subscription in 2016 and now boasts 19.3 million unique users!

Today, the idea that *SELF* is number one is pretty much taken for granted.

But where does God fit into all this?

If, for example, I am supposed to be able to figure out my problems myself and if I am the ultimate judge of what's best for me and if I answer to no one and if my top goal is to become *self-actualized*, then where does Jesus matter?

Why did Jesus have to come to earth to pay for our sins?

---

[7] https://en.wikipedia.org/wiki/Self_(magazine).

In fact, why would I even care about God? If *self* is number one, then God is irrelevant.

According to Maslow's theories, a person cannot be reasonably expected to move to a higher level of thinking or behaving until they have sufficiently mastered their current level.

If I can't be expected to move to the 'morality' need area until after all my other needs are met, then all the other things become most important.

I am excused from all other obligations because (the reasoning goes) '*I have needs.*

If I have 'needs' that aren't met, then I can't be expected to serve others—God or you—until those needs are met.

This kind of thinking has affected the church in a big way. For example, we've taken one of the key teachings of Jesus and turned it around.

"Teacher, which is the most important commandment in the law of Moses?"

> Jesus replied, "'You must love the Lord your God with all your heart, all your soul, and all your mind.' This is the first and greatest commandment. A second is equally important: 'Love your neighbor as yourself.' The entire law and all the demands of the prophets are based on these two commandments." (Matthew 22:36–40)

Because of an emphasis on "self" in our culture, we've taken Jesus's clear intent—*loving God* with everything we've got and *loving others* similarly—and turned it around as a "command" to *love ourselves!*

This then leads us to excuse our fixation on ourselves and gives us cover for not going out of our way—for God or for others.

There is simply *no way* you or I will ever be passionately committed to God and to truly be "salt" and "light" (see chapter 1) if we keep justifying a focus on "self."

Make no mistake about it: the Bible—both OT and NT—is filled with teachings to give up ourselves, deny ourselves, put others—especially God—before ourselves, and so on.

If "self" is allowed to be number one, then these teachings are made irrelevant.

> Then he said to the crowd, "If any of you wants to be my follower, you must turn from your selfish ways, take up your cross daily, and follow me. If you try to hang on to your life, you will lose it. But if you give up your life for my sake, you will save it." (Luke 9:23–24)

If we are to be Christ followers, then we are to model His love—for the Heavenly Father first and all others second.

If we are truly Christ followers, then we live by His example.

> "Don't be selfish; don't try to impress others. Be humble, thinking of others as better than yourselves. Don't look out only for your own interests, but take an interest in others, too. You must have the same attitude that Christ Jesus had." (Philippians 2:3–5)

One of the keys to becoming a Christ follower is this attitude of self-denial, followed by *actions* that back it up:

> "You must have the same attitude that Christ Jesus had. Though he was God, he did not think of equality with God as something to cling to. Instead, he gave up his divine privileges; he took the humble position of a slave and was born as a human being. When he appeared in human form, he humbled himself in obedience to God and died a criminal's death on a cross." (Philippians 2:5–8)

We are called to follow Jesus—in attitude, in word, and in action.

Think about it: if *anyone* had the right to be self-centered and *all about Himself*, it was Jesus!

What did He model instead? Self-sacrificing love.
In fact, that was one of the keys to God showing love to us.

> "God so loved the world that He gave his only begotten Son, that whoever would believe in Him would not perish, but would have everlasting life." (John 3:16).

That word *love* is the translation of the Greek word *agape*. It means "sacrificial love"; gracious, generous, and over-the-top love; and speaks most clearly to God's love for us—accompanied by His willingness to sacrifice for us.

So in many respects, the most Christlike love there is is *self-sacrificial love*. I would even say it is virtually impossible to be following Christ and be selfish at the same time.

Note that I did not say a person who is a Christ follower would never be selfish, simply that being selfish is *not* being Christlike and that is, after all, what we say we're about.

Yet "self" as an idol is very real in the church today.
Does *love of self*, or *selfishness*, come between me and God?
Do I give to my *self* God's rightful place?

For far too many of us, the answer is yes!
How does this show?
How do I know if I am struggling with this?
How do you know if *you* are?

There are several ways.

1) <u>I use God</u> to get my needs met.

If I *demand* that He make me happy, content, secure, healthy, wealthy, and wise then turn my back if He doesn't …

If you find yourself getting angry at God and saying something like "Forget it! Following God doesn't help," you may be guilty of the idolatry of self.

Remember the story of Job.

He was a good man commended as such by God Himself! Yet Satan went to God and said,

> "Does Job fear God for nothing?" Satan replied. "Have you not put a hedge around him and his household and everything he has? You have blessed the work of his hands, so that his flocks and herds are spread throughout the land. But now stretch out your hand and strike everything he has, and he will surely curse you to your face." (Job 1:9–11)

Satan was implying that the only reason Job was so "righteous" was because of the protection and blessing God had given to him. If the Lord took that away, Job would respond by unbelief.

> The LORD said to Satan, "Very well, then, everything he has is in your power, but on the man himself do not lay a finger." (Job 1:12)

God gave him permission, and all hell broke loose upon Job. *Literally!* First, Job's oxen, then his sheep, then his camels—and virtually all his servants watching them—were killed or stolen. And then the worst news of all: All of Job's children were having a get-together at the oldest brother's house when a great wind came along and caused the house to collapse. All his children were killed!

This was a *terrible* series of events that would cause anyone to struggle hugely with the Lord!

But not Job!

His response?

> "Job stood up and tore his robe in grief. Then he shaved his head and fell to the ground to worship. He said, "I came naked from my mother's womb, and I will be naked when I leave. The Lord gave me what I had, and the Lord has taken it away. Praise the name of the Lord!" In all of this, Job did not sin by blaming God. (Job 1:20–22)

He "fell to the ground to worship"? Wow!

Another day, Satan comes before God and God says,

> "Have you considered my servant Job? There is no one on earth like him; he is blameless and upright, a man who fears God and shuns evil. And he still maintains his integrity, though you incited me against him to ruin him without any reason."
>
> "Skin for skin!" Satan replied. "A man will give all he has for his own life. But now stretch out your hand and strike his flesh and bones, and he will surely curse you to your face."
>
> The Lord said to Satan, "Very well, then, he is in your hands; but you must spare his life." (Job 2:3–6)

So Satan left the Lord's presence and struck him, head to toe, with boils. Painful, puss-filled, oozing boils.

Yuk—and ouch!

Job's wife had seen enough! She said, "Are you still trying to maintain your integrity? Curse God and die."

Let's be done with this and get it over with!

His wife was in the 'I'll serve God as long as it works for me' camp.

> But Job replied, "You talk like a foolish woman. Should we accept only good things from the hand of God and never anything bad?" (Job 2:9–11)

The rest of the book (it's a long one) consists of Job dealing with his friends, who assume that there must be some sin that he has not confessed and that's why God is sending this "punishment" upon him.

Eventually, Job and the Lord 'discuss' it, and Job reaffirms his trust in the Lord. God blesses and restores him.

Using God to get my needs met is *not* the way to go!

2) I exalt my own opinion on the way "things should be" over His Word's clear teaching.

> Who are you, a mere human being, to argue with God? (Romans 9:20)

Remember also that this is precisely the line of reasoning that led Adam and Eve into sin!

Genesis says,

> "The serpent was the shrewdest of all the wild animals the Lord God had made. One day he asked the woman, "Did God really say you must not eat the fruit from any of the trees in the garden?" "Of course we may eat fruit from the trees in the garden," the woman replied. "It's only the fruit from the tree in the middle of the garden that we are not allowed to eat.

God said, 'You must not eat it or even touch it; if you do, you will die.'"

"You won't die!" the serpent replied to the woman. "God knows that your eyes will be opened as soon as you eat it, and you will be like God, knowing both good and evil."

The woman was convinced. She saw that the tree was beautiful and its fruit looked delicious, and she wanted the wisdom it would give her. So she took some of the fruit and ate it. Then she gave some to her husband, who was with her, and he ate it, too. At that moment their eyes were opened, and they suddenly felt shame at their nakedness." (Genesis 3:1–7)

The devil, our spiritual enemy, is *still* at work and is still trying to get us to question God's character, wisdom, love, and holiness.

He is *still* trying to get us to rebel against God, promising freedom and enlightenment and even success and popularity when we follow our own way—and the ways (and *wisdom*) of this world—and rejecting God's Lordship over us.

Our world plays into this by trying, with its *self*-centered philosophy, to get us to subject God to our own feelings, our own opinions, and our own "wisdom."

And, to the extent that we buy into it, we are deceived.

We should *resist* the power of our culture, with its self-centered philosophy and morality, and instead, we must *engage* in the battle for our own hearts and minds—and those of every Christ follower we know.

Instead of giving in,

"We demolish arguments and every pretension that sets itself up against the knowledge of God, and we take captive every thought to make it obedient to Christ." (2 Corinthians 10:5)

3) <u>I try to make God prove Himself</u> to me.

In effect, I exalt myself over God, and I think as though *He* has to earn *my* acceptance!

Some of us start our journey of faith that way—asking God to prove to us that He's there, to give us a sign, etc., and He graciously does so.

However, if you are still putting God on *probation*, demanding that He continue to prove Himself to you, there's a good bet that you've put "self" in His rightful place and are guilty of spiritual idolatry.

So if I'm struggling with the spiritual idol of self, I might be

- using God to meet my needs
- exalting my own opinion over His word and His wisdom
- making Him *prove Himself* to me

Another indication that I might be struggling with the idol of self.

4) <u>I try to manipulate God</u> into my way of thinking.

Idolatry of self really makes me and my desires number 1. It says, "I deserve …" a lot!

If you find yourself praying for things you've "earned" or you think God's failure to answer your prayers your way is unfair, you may be guilty of the idolatry of self.

That reminds me of a passage I read recently.

> "You should know this, Timothy, that in the last days there will be very difficult times. For people will love

only themselves and their money. They will be boa~~ and proud, scoffing at God, disobedient to th~~ parents, and ungrateful. They will consider nothing sacred. They will be unloving and unforgiving; they will slander others and have no self-control. They will be cruel and hate what is good. They will betray their friends, be reckless, be puffed up with pride, and love pleasure rather than God. They will act religious, but they will reject the power that could make them godly. Stay away from people like that!" (2 Timothy 3:1–5)

Lovers of themselves and their money, boastful, proud, disobedient, and ungrateful.

Unloving, unforgiving, slanderous, no self-control, and cruel. Does that sound a lot like our culture today?

It does to me!

5) Finally, another sign that I may be struggling with the spiritual idolatry of self is I find myself telling God no in response to specific leading.

Perhaps He's leading us to have a conversation with a friend about Him. Maybe He's leading us to get baptized. He may be leading us to give financially to the church or some cause.

If I find myself saying no, it may be that I'm not only struggling with my faith (natural growth process) but that I may have some self-centered spiritual idolatry going on!

Remember Jonah. He was called, specifically, by God to go to Nineveh to preach against it. He refused and sailed the opposite way. He knew those people were evil!

What was Jonah's reason?

It was not fear or intimidation but that He knew God's character, and he knew God would have mercy on the people if they repented, and Jonah wanted them punished!

Later, that's precisely what happened, and Jonah was ticked! Jonah prayed to the Lord, "Isn't this what I said, Lord, when I was still at home? That is what I tried to forestall by fleeing to Tarshish. I knew that you are a gracious and compassionate God, slow to anger and abounding in love, a God who relents from sending calamity. Now, Lord, take away my life, for it is better for me to die than to live." (Jonah 4:1–3)

Jonah *knew* God would have mercy on them and forgive them, and he thought he would rather die than live when Ninevites would be forgiven!

Jonah was so negative against the Ninevites that he even knowingly turned his back on a direct call of God!

The point in all this is that You and I are *not* God! We do not have the right to set the standard or to change the standards. We have no power to do so either!

> "But the time is coming—indeed it's here now—when true worshipers will worship the Father in spirit and in truth. The Father is looking for those who will worship him that way. For God is Spirit, so those who worship him must worship in spirit and in truth." (John 4:23–24)

As I wrote previously, I believe that our culture is getting darker and more anti-Christ.

It may very well continue its march toward compromise and rebellion against God, but we *cannot* let that happen within the church! Instead, we must recommit ourselves to standing up and willingly submitting ourselves to Him.

It is time, that we "live clean, innocent lives as children of God, shining like bright lights in a world full of crooked and perverse people. Hold firmly to the word of life" (Philippians 2:15–16).

We know that doing so leads to true life, despite what our enemy tries to get us to believe.

Remember Jesus said, "The thief comes only to steal, kill and destroy. I have come that they [His followers] might have life; Life to the full!" (John 10:10).

I began this chapter by stating my belief that one of the most impactful of the "American idols" is "self." Self-love has been so overused that it's corrupted everything from our understanding of God and how we relate to Him to our following Jesus and loving our neighbors—even how we view ourselves.

There *is* a better way! It is the way of love. But it is the way of *divine* love—not human or self-centered love.

Love that puts others first, starting with the love of God, followed by the love of others. "Love is patient and kind. Love is not jealous or boastful or proud or rude. It does not demand its own way. It is not irritable, and it keeps no record of being wronged. It does not rejoice about injustice but rejoices whenever the truth wins out. Love never gives up, never loses faith, is always hopeful, and endures through every circumstance. Love never fails." (1 Corinthians 13:4–8)

Today, right now, if we are realizing that we have compromised our understanding of love and have put our *selves* in God's rightful place of priority in our hearts, that we have been guilty of spiritual idolatry.

Let us repent, turn back, get on a different road, and go back to what we knew at first.

Loving God means radical commitment to follow Him, living according to His Word, the Bible, and living it out in our relationships to this world.

It means loving Him first and foremost and loving others similarly. It means sacrificing self on the altar of real faith. It's part of what makes Christ followers so different in this world and enables us to be "salt" and "light" in this world. We dare not compromise that!

CHAPTER 3
THE IDOL OF "STUFF"

I LOVED SUNDAYS GROWING UP.

One of the things I loved was breakfast. My mom would make lots of scrambled eggs, sausage, bacon, toast, and orange juice. It would rival any restaurant. That's for sure!

Another thing I remember about Sundays was my dad reading the Sunday paper in the afternoon, after church.

When I was little, I went right to the comics. Soon after that, I went right to the sports section. A little later, after I had a job, I started to look right for the ads. I wanted to see what was on sale that I *needed*. (Of course, the reality was that I didn't *need* any of it. I sure did *want* some of it though!) Whether it was the latest CD, some stereo equipment, movies, clothes—the list could go on. When I looked at those Sunday ads, my eyes would light up, and my heart would burn to buy something!

Later, after I started dating Lori and we got married, we would often go to a local mall and engage in an activity that makes very little rational sense: window shopping.

AMERICAN IDOLS

This phenomenon is unique to our culture, I think—or at least to "wealthy" cultures. Think about it: going to a place that has nothing but stuff to buy—even when you have no money and no need to buy anything—is irrational! It sets us up for frustration. It sets us up for failure!

I remember once, early in our marriage, Lori and I met her parents for lunch at a restaurant in a mall after church. We had a nice visit and a good lunch, then we walked around the mall—you guessed it—window shopping.

When Lori came to a women's clothing store (I can hear all the men groaning with me, cuz they know what it means: waiting and spending), she found a sweater she really liked. She tried it on, and it looked good on her; she's beautiful in anything, of course. She wanted to buy it, but I said, "We can't, honey. We haven't got the money." She wanted it anyway, but with her parents looking on, I said, "No, we just can't." She took it off, put it back, and began to walk out of the store.

You know that vibe you get when someone is mad at you but they don't tell you that they're mad? If you try to hold their hand, it's rigid. If you try to carry on a conversation, but it's a series of one-word answers. I was definitely getting that vibe. Soon after, we went home. When we walked in the door, she went right to the bedroom and slammed (OK, *closed firmly and quickly*) the door.

I let her have some time, and later she came out in tears! I couldn't believe it!

She apologized but said that she was struggling because of the sweater. She had pretty much always been able to get the things (especially clothing) she wanted in her parents' house, and now the reality of early marriage was hitting her. We talked about it, prayed, and were fine. But the sheer power of *stuff* was amazing.

I want to be clear this wasn't just her problem, and it wasn't just about clothes. My 'stuff' issues have a lot more to do with technology, sports gear, etc., but it's still just stuff.

Stuff is a pretty big deal in our culture. Accumulating more stuff, newer stuff, and better stuff drives a lot of us. We tell ourselves, "If I just had more stuff, I'd be happy!'

Have you ever said anything like these statements that I've said?

- If I just had a *bigger house,* I'd be happy.
- If I just had a *newer car,* I'd be happy.
- If I just had *newer clothes,* I'd be happy.
- If I just had a *bigger TV,* I'd be happy.
- If we could just afford a *nicer vacation*, I'd be happy.
- If I just had *more money* left at the end of the month, I'd be happy.

None of us would probably say, "I need more stuff," but we often act like it. And in a sense, the American economy is based on it. Newspaper ads, commercials, and pop-up ads on social media are crucial parts of what drives our economic engine! Why? Because they get one to think, *I need that stuff!*

If retailers can get me convinced that I need their stuff in order to be fulfilled and happy, then they've won half the battle.

If I combine that with the "idol of self" from the last chapter, then I can easily convince myself that not only do I *want* that new thing, but I *deserve* that new thing. And then it's all over but the purchase.

And if I don't have the money to purchase, but I have access to credit, then we say, "Go for it!"

My kids loved watching *VeggieTales* when they were younger. One of their favorite episodes is "Madame Blueberry." (I know blueberries are not veggies, but that's not the point. Work with me here!) In that episode, Madame Blueberry is discontented because she sees on the TV that there are new things she can buy, and when she looks around at her stuff that is in fine condition but not "new"), she feels "blue."

Fortunately for her, a "StuffMart" moves into the neighborhood and her worries seem to be over, because she can now buy almost any stuff that she wants—and they'll even open a credit account for her! It's a great lesson about thankfulness and contentment, but in the lead up to it, Bob (the tomato and host of the series) asks Larry (the cucumber and cohost) how much stuff he will need to make himself happy. Larry's answer: "I don't know. How much stuff is there?"

It's a great answer, and it speaks to the way we tend to live: If there's more/newer/nicer stuff to have, I <u>need it</u> in order to be happy. Why is it these *things*—stuff—can have such power over us? Why has "retail therapy" become your preferred method of treatment for depression or stress for so many of us?

Seriously, men, how many fishing lures do you need? How many jerseys? Do you *really* need the newest smartphone? Is it *really* that important that you have the biggest-screen TV or that newer and more powerful tool?

Women, seriously, do you really *need* that many purses? Or shoes? Do you really need a new outfit *just because*? How much jewelry is really necessary?

For all of us, is it *possible*—just possible—that we've bought into another "American idol"?

Remember the definition of idolatry: worship, service, or devotion to something that is not God, as though it were God; giving God's rightful place of ultimate devotion to someone or something else. Is it possible that we've made stuff an idol in our lives? Is it possible that we've bought into the lie that says, "If we had more stuff, we could be happy"?

The apostle John wrote,

> "Do not love this world nor the things it offers you, for when you love the world, you do not have the love of the Father in you. For the world offers only a craving for physical pleasure, a craving for everything we see, and pride in our achievements and possessions. These are not from the Father, but are from this world. And

this world is fading away, along with everything that people crave. But anyone who does what pleases God will live forever." (1 John 2:15–17)

The world offers us cravings, whiffs, and phantoms.

It promises satisfaction and contentment through stuff, but these things are (to use John's words) "fading away." Only the *eternal* things we pay attention to are going to last.

Jesus said it this way:

> "Don't store up treasures here on earth, where moths eat them and rust destroys them, and where thieves break in and steal. Store your treasures in heaven, where moths and rust cannot destroy, and thieves do not break in and steal. Wherever your treasure is, there the desires of your heart will also be … No one can serve two masters. For you will hate one and love the other; you will be devoted to one and despise the other. You cannot serve both God and money." (Matthew 6:19–24)

So what is this 'idol' we're talking about? It's the "idol" of materialism.

What is materialism?

Preoccupying or obsessing over material things, usually with rejection of spiritual and intellectual priorities. It's the love of the material over the spiritual. The belief that the only real stuff of life is material—*stuff!* Things that are spiritual and emotional aren't real or at least aren't worth pursuing.

Ultimately, we are material beings.

Madonna famously sang, "We're living in a material world, and I am a material girl." In that song, she was embracing the fact that men would spend money buying her things to win her affection and she was working that in her own favor! What is that called? Greed.

The insatiable appetite for more (in this case, more stuff) is huge! And our world encourages it!

Jesus warned us against it.

> "Then he said, "Beware! Guard against every kind of greed. Life is not measured by how much you own."
>
> Then he told them a story: "A rich man had a fertile farm that produced fine crops. He said to himself, 'What should I do? I don't have room for all my crops.' Then he said, 'I know! I'll tear down my barns and build bigger ones. Then I'll have room enough to store all my wheat and other goods. And I'll sit back and say to myself, "My friend, you have enough stored away for years to come. Now take it easy! Eat, drink, and be merry!"'
>
> "But God said to him, 'You fool! You will die this very night. Then who will get everything you worked for?'
>
> Yes, a person is a fool to store up earthly wealth but not have a rich relationship with God." (Luke 12:15–21)

People who have lots but just want more are said to be greedy, and this is one of the many areas where we can easily spot it in *other* people but may be blind to it in ourselves.

For example, I know people who have moved from one house to another, always getting bigger, newer, more expensive homes. When they finally settled in one of those, they actually went out and bought a second home.

They have very small families who are scattered all over the place and are rarely together in either of these large, expensive homes.

I can easily spot it in *them*.

Yet when we bought our home about sixteen years ago—in the neighborhood we'd been wanting, the house we'd had our eyes on—it didn't take me long to think (as I was taking a walk in the neighborhood) that we'd made the wrong purchase and that I would rather have had one of the bigger homes a couple of blocks away.

I'll admit it: I struggle with *perspective* at times, and I know it!

I have been blessed in many, many ways, yet *if I choose to*, I can always find things to complain about, and I can list many ways that others have it better than I do. I can be greedy! Probably you can too!

Greed has nothing to do with the level of our wealth. We tend to think of the "greedy" rich guy who only got that way (we think) because he lied, cheated, stole, or stabbed people in the back. We think of the person who always has to have something new: newer car, newer (bigger) house, newest phone, latest TV, more clothes, more shoes, more purses, etc.

Those guys (and gals) do exist, but just because a person has a lot of money does not mean they're all cheats or they're all materialistic and greedy. Some of the most generous people I've known have been wealthy; some of the stingiest, greediest, and most selfish people I've known have very little.

Having money doesn't make you materialistic any more than *not* having money makes you spiritual. Make no mistake: those who have very little *can* be *very* materialistic, stingy, selfish, and greedy. The amount of money you have does not change that.

The truth is we often look at stuff as the key to our contentment, happiness, and sense of well-being in our culture.

A few examples are the following:

Happy Meals

Happy Meals first came out in 1979 as a convenient box with a drink, burger, fries, and a toy. The idea was to make it easy for moms to keep their kids content and get them fed more easily. I would bet that virtually every American has at some point had a Happy Meal. How many of you were ever made *truly* happy by the toy?

I've heard children complain about the toys, either because they already have one, they missed the toy they really wanted, etc. Happy meals became more "Complaining Meals." Ultimately, it seems, when you feed a child's desire for more stuff, he or she doesn't become more content; he or she becomes less content.

But it's not only children.

Magazine Sweepstakes

How many of you have ever entered magazine sweepstakes? Why? I used to enter, taking care to put all the stamps in just the right place. I'd even buy *one* magazine, just because I did not believe that "No purchase necessary" line. I'd think of all the good, noble, Christ-honoring ways I could spend that money—and then get bummed when I didn't win.

Finally I realized that I was actually *worshipping at the wrong altar*. I was asking God, in essence, to bless my appetites—my desires!

Have you ever found yourself doing that kind of thing?

Super Lotto

State lotteries and casinos have become wildly popular; each year *billions* of dollars are given to these in order to win *millions* of dollars in cash and prizes. Why? Because we think it will make us happy and content.

The writers of scripture—some of whom were wealthy—knew better.

> "Give me an eagerness for your laws
> rather than a love for money!
> Turn my eyes from worthless things,
> and give me life through your word." (Psalm 119:36–37)

Going through life with the goal of getting more stuff may drive us, and we may become successful in the eyes of this world. Ultimately, most know that cannot satisfy. Rather, we should be going through life with a desire to know and love God more and a willingness—even a commitment—to serve God and His kingdom with our material resources. Then we will be on the road to true contentment.

The apostle Paul knew this well. He had been around lots of powerful, influential, and wealthy people all his life, but he knew that these things—*these materialistic things*—cannot touch the heart and cannot ultimately satisfy. In the words of Philosopher Blaise Paschal:

> "What else does this craving, and this helplessness, proclaim but that there was once in man a true happiness, of which all that now remains is the empty print and trace?
>
> This he tries in vain to fill with everything around him, seeking in things that are not there the help he cannot find in those that are, though none can help, since this infinite abyss can be filled only with an infinite and immutable object; in other words by God himself."[8]

---

[8] Blaise Pascal's *Pensees* (New York; Penguin Books, 1966).

The apostle Paul said it this way:

> "Yet true godliness with contentment is itself great wealth. After all, we brought nothing with us when we came into the world, and we can't take anything with us when we leave it. So if we have enough food and clothing, let us be content.
>
> But people who long to be rich fall into temptation and are trapped by many foolish and harmful desires that plunge them into ruin and destruction. For the love of money is the root of all kinds of evil. And some people, craving money, have wandered from the true faith and pierced themselves with many sorrows." (1 Timothy 6:6–10)

Instead of making it our goal to become rich, we—as followers of Jesus Christ—should make it our goal to be used by the Lord for His purposes in this world—in part, by giving Him control over our finances, our purchases, and even the things we set before our eyes.

> "Teach those who are rich in this world not to be proud and not to trust in their money, which is so unreliable. Their trust should be in God, who richly gives us all we need for our enjoyment. Tell them to use their money to do good. They should be rich in good works and generous to those in need, always being ready to share with others. By doing this they will be storing up their treasure as a good foundation for the future so that they may experience true life." (1 Timothy 6:17–19)

Maybe you think these verses and this teaching isn't about you because you aren't *rich*.

Well, if you have clean water to drink, if you have a place to sleep, if you have more than one pair of shoes or more than one pair of clean clothes, you are far richer than the vast majority of the world's population!

Instead of thinking that *other people* need to listen to this, apply it to your own heart. What then should be our attitude toward material possessions and finances? Should we feel guilty about the stuff we own and the money we have? Should we sell everything and give it to the poor?

Maybe…But not necessarily! However, we *should* let God change our perspective and our value of stuff.

We should let Him change us to give us a new and better way, including the following:

1. Accept it as a blessing.

   "Don't be deceived, my dear brothers. Every good and perfect gift is from above, coming down from the Father of the heavenly lights." (James 1:16–17)

When my wife and I moved our two kids to seminary in 1991, we knew there would be challenges. We did not know how difficult it would be from a stuff standpoint. The reality of life in seminary became a cold slap in the face soon after we moved though. The seminary had a room, called the "blessing room," where people would donate items—mostly clothing—to the school for the students and their families. When that first winter rolled around and our kids had grown out of their coats, we found some—we were blessed—through the blessing room. But I have to confess it was very hard to go to the blessing room for the first time. It felt like begging, it felt like failure, and it felt very humbling. But it was good for me!

I had to learn about God's desire to bless His children, about my own pride and materialism, and about the church and how they can bless each other when they get "self" out of the way. We soon began to check—and to contribute to—the blessing room regularly!

2. Turn it back over to Him.

We simply must get over the mindset that our culture promotes, which is 'This stuff is *mine!* I *deserve* it!' The blessings we enjoy come from the Lord, and the best way to handle them is to give thanks for them and hold to them very loosely so that if God asks you to give something up, you are willing to do so instantly.

Think of the early church.

In the book of Acts, we read (2:42–47) that the early believers had a good handle on this and that, when a need arose, "All the believers were united and shared everything. They would sell pieces of property and possessions and distribute the proceeds to everyone who needed them."

There was no *'It's mine'* mindset. There was love for the Lord and each other and a willingness to submit to the Lord and His will for the church. We need that again today!

So what is to be our attitude toward the stuff we possess instead? Surrender and worship. Hold it loosely, be ready and willing to freely give it when God prompts you, and worship Him with all your heart and mind!

3. Put it to use for His purposes.

> "Now I want you to know, dear brothers and sisters, what God in his kindness has done through the churches in Macedonia. They are being tested by many troubles, and they are very poor. But they are

also filled with abundant joy, which has overflowed in rich generosity.

For I can testify that they gave not only what they could afford, but far more. And they did it of their own free will. They begged us again and again for the privilege of sharing in the gift for the believers in Jerusalem. They even did more than we had hoped, for their first action was to give themselves to the Lord and to us, just as God wanted them to do." (2 Corinthians 8:1–5)

Again, the early church had something that we can learn from. When the church in Macedonia (a poor church, from the world's perspective) heard about persecution in the church at Jerusalem and the resulting (legit) "need" that existed there, they gave what they had—above and beyond expectation. They did it out of love, concern, and faith.

4. Refuse to be conformed to this world's standards of "wealth."

Don't buy into the lies that say, "He who dies with the most toys wins." No one ever came to the end of their lives having turned their backs on God, family, and other relationships and having pursued *stuff* and been glad they did!

This world will tell you that you need stuff to be content, successful, and happy. This world lies.

> "Do not be conformed to the standards of this world [including how it views wealth and stuff], but be transformed by the renewing of your mind." (Romans 12:2)

5. Let God transform you by transforming how closely you hold on to the stuff He blesses you with!

"Remember this—a farmer who plants only a few seeds will get a small crop. But the one who plants generously will get a generous crop. You must each decide in your heart how much to give. And don't give reluctantly or in response to pressure. For God loves a person who gives cheerfully. And God will generously provide all you need. Then you will always have everything you need and plenty left over to share with others. As the Scriptures say,

"They share freely and give generously to the poor. Their good deeds will be remembered forever."

For God is the one who provides seed for the farmer and then bread to eat. In the same way, he will provide and increase your resources and then produce a great harvest of generosity in you. Yes, you will be enriched in every way so that you can always be generous." (2 Corinthians 9:6–11)

When we are convinced that God knows our needs, God can and will meet our needs, and God wants to bless us, His children; we can have confidence to let go and to be generous to His work.

The Importance of Giving

The tithe is something that many churches shy away from speaking about because they don't want to be perceived of as greedy or to be accused of only wanting my money. God speaks of a tithe (which, incidentally, is not just any amount given but 10 percent—the *first* 10 percent—of your earnings) not because He wants you to "earn" anything but because it's one of the biggest "idols" in our world—our trust in material wealth—and *it must be slain!*

If we are going to grow in faith, in love, and contentment, we simply must get a handle on our attitude about our stuff. We must trust God more than we trust our pension, our 401(k), our savings account, our credit cards, etc.

That's why God takes an unprecedented step of asking us to test Him!

> "Should people cheat God? Yet you have cheated me!
>
> "But you ask, 'What do you mean? When did we ever cheat you?'
>
> "You have cheated me of the tithes and offerings due to me. You are under a curse, for your whole nation has been cheating me. Bring all the tithes into the storehouse so there will be enough food in my Temple. If you do," says the Lord of Heaven's Armies, "I will open the windows of heaven for you. I will pour out a blessing so great you won't have enough room to take it in!
>
> <u>Try it! Put me to the test!</u> Your crops will be abundant, for I will guard them from insects and disease. Your grapes will not fall from the vine before they are ripe," says the Lord of Heaven's Armies. "Then all nations will call you blessed, for your land will be such a delight," says the Lord of Heaven's Armies."
> (Malachi 3:8–12)

Is this still true for today? Some disagree, but I believe it is. God wants us to tithe *not* because he needs the money but because it's good for *our* development. It helps us to hold on loosely to the stuff God has blessed us with! It helps us each time to reaffirm our faith in God—as the giver of all good gifts—and our willingness to follow His will and worship Him.

Does 10 percent seem *way too hard* for you to imagine? Try this: *Start* at what you give now. Loose change? 1 percent? 5 percent? Whatever it is, *add 1 percent for one month*, and give it first—before you buy groceries, get gas, pay bills, etc. Give it prayerfully, as an act of faith, and trust God. He will meet your needs, and you will learn that He is faithful. Give it every time you get paid. Then next month, *add another percent*. Give it prayerfully, as an act of faith, but continue to give it *first*. The month after that, add another percent, and so on.

> Watch God work! Watch Him move and meet needs!
> He will be faithful in this, no doubt.

If we want to defeat the "idol" of stuff in our lives, we must

- accept the stuff you have as a blessing from God
- hold onto it loosely and release it back to Him
- *not* allow it to become an idol that comes between you and Him
- ask God to show you this and to help you be more generous—more "kingdom minded"—about your stuff

And God will do powerful things through you and me! In this way, the Lord will enable you and me to "cast down this idol" and to live in freedom!

CHAPTER 4
THE IDOL OF POPULARITY

A True Story of Two Young People

ON ONE SIDE OF TOWN, A FOURTEEN-YEAR-OLD BOY IS TRANSFERRING from a small private school to a much larger public one, where he knows exactly *one* person well. He is shy, short, and a bit intimidated. One of his main goals is to be accepted—and to not get beat up!

On the other side of town, a fourteen-year-old girl is transferring to a new school too—and moving to an entirely new community. She also wants to be accepted. She is a bit shy and wonders what the new classmates will think of her.

The boy gets introduced by his one friend to some of the "popular" people in school. He wonders whether or not they'll let him in. After all, he's fairly quiet, not very athletic, and shorter than most his age.

The girl, on the other hand, goes in with some apprehension, but much confidence also. She knows that she won't end up "best friends" with everyone but assumes that she'll find some good friends at her new school.

The boy has a stroke of good luck. One of the 'popular' girls realizes that he looks a lot like one of the coolest, most desirable boys in the school! This leads to instant invitations to early school year parties, compliments from random kids in the hallways, and even an invitation to *go with* one of the most popular, best-looking girls in the school! What good fortune! The boy goes from anonymity to popularity within one week! He is not only *accepted* but welcomed and sought out!

And really, all he has to do is to compromise a bit of his character. After all, the 'popular' people also smoke, drink, smoke pot, and do other drugs. They also look down on other groups—the less desirable ones—and don't associate with them.

The boy has a crisis on his hands. Who will he be? Will he continue with the values he was raised with, even if it means giving up his newfound celebrity, or will he compromise those values in order to ride the wave of popularity?

The crisis is over almost before it starts. The boy completely caves, turning his back—in a deliberate decision to seek popularity at all costs—on everything he's been taught to that point about quality of character.

On the other side of town, the girl is faced with similar choices. Will she seek to fit in with the "popular" people at any cost? Will she remain true to her beliefs and upbringing, even if it means rejection? Again, the battle is over almost before it starts. She unequivocally commits to the values of her core. She reaffirms those beliefs and sticks by them, not obnoxiously but assertively.

Fast-forward four years.

Both are wildly popular in their schools. Both are on homecoming court, and both are sought out for friendship and attention. But there's a big difference.

The girl has her core—her principles, beliefs, character, and self-image—intact while the boy has compromised so much that he is a mere shell of who he once was.

Even at a young age, he has 'worshipped' at the idol of popularity and has paid for it dearly. To be sure, on the surface, he looks great. He is successful, good-looking, and well-liked by kids from all groups—the jocks, the partiers, the brains, and the motorheads. Most importantly, the girls really like him! Even the teachers like him.

He should be happy, right? His goal was met. Popularity has been attained—wildly so!

So why does he feel so empty?

The scriptures say, "Fear of man will prove to be a snare, but whoever trusts in the Lord is kept safe" (Proverbs 29:25 NIV).

Fear of man in this context can be a literal fear of what people can do to me physically—that is, how they can beat me, injure me, even kill me.

However, fear of man can be much broader than fear of physical harm. It can be an unhealthy fixation on others' opinions of me and my willingness to give them too much influence over my thoughts, behavior, and beliefs—all in the pursuit of popularity. And it always leads to a hollowed-out core.

A quick survey of those movie stars and musicians who started out innocently and idealistically only to end up compromising their core—for continued popularity—shows the truth: Britney Spears, Lindsay Lohan, Miley Cyrus, and Vanessa Hudgens. And the jury's still out on Justin Bieber and Selena Gomez.

The truth is that for entertainers to remain 'relevant' and thus earn big dollars, receive invitations to the 'right' parties, receive offers of quality scripts, and receive invitations to appear on the big talk shows, they *must* stay in the limelight. That means, in most cases, that they have to push the envelope in their fashion, their morality, the roles they play, etc.

Each one of them has a choice to make: maintain their integrity and moral center or give in and remain popular. It is the rare Hollywood star who can do both.

In most cases, it appears as though they regard worldly success and popularity as too great to pass up and they give in. Whatever good morals they once had, whatever beliefs they started out with, often gets traded in for bigger paychecks and more headlines.

Just look at the magazine rack in a typical grocery store checkout lane. Real-life scandals (in addition to the made-up ones) seem to be the one thing they all have in common. However, for many of them, it seems that the only thing worse than a life full of drama, scandal, broken relationships, and pain is a life of irrelevance and anonymity.

You and I may never be 'stars' in this sense, and our personal relationships may never make the headlines of the hottest magazines, but we still face this harsh reality: too much value of the opinions of others can lead us to decisions that will ruin our lives.

Whether you're like the ninth-grade boy who basically sold out for popularity or the stars who get paid millions of dollars but have no peace, no real satisfaction, and no way of knowing whether or not anybody *really* loves them, the truth is this: they are often hollow at their core and their hearts are aching for real friends, real acceptance, and real love.

So where is it found? How can we avoid the pain and misery of a life ruined by the idol of popularity?

By finding ourselves, and our core, with God!

The Lord—who created us and knows us better than anyone—is the only One worthy of our worship and attention!

> "You made all the delicate, inner parts of my body
> and knit me together in my mother's womb.
> Thank you for making me so wonderfully complex!
> Your workmanship is marvelous—how well I know it.

You watched me as I was being formed in utter seclusion,
as I was woven together in the dark of the womb.
You saw me before I was born.
Every day of my life was recorded in your book.
Every moment was laid out
before a single day had passed.

How precious are your thoughts about me, O God.
They cannot be numbered!
I can't even count them;
they outnumber the grains of sand!
And when I wake up,
you are still with me!" (Psalm 139:13–18)

The Lord designed each one of us to be perfectly unique, perfectly *us!*

You will never be duplicated. Your DNA, your personality, your experiences, your passions, tastes, preferences, education, and experiences will never be duplicated in another person (no matter what scientists are able to do with "cloning.") In this sense, you *are* special!

Ironically, the very things that many in this world are after—love, success, meaning, and purpose—are not found in the things of this world alone but only in a relationship with the Lord.

That's part of the reason the apostle John wrote,

> "Do not love this world nor the things it offers you, for when you love the world, you do not have the love of the Father in you. For the world offers only a craving for physical pleasure, a craving for everything we see, and pride in our achievements and possessions. These are not from the Father, but are from this world. And this world is fading away, along with everything that

people crave. But anyone who does what pleases God will live forever." (1 John 2:15–17)

The things [this world] offers you are temporary, at best.

The Lord, however, offers us eternal love, acceptance, and meaning. These things will never be taken away—no matter what we look like, no matter how we age, and no matter how "popular" we are.

This changes everything!

If we really let this sink in, and if we really understood this, it would dramatically change our view of ourselves, giving us freedom and liberation! It would also change the fears we have of the opinions of others and the power that their threats of rejection have to control us. We would discover power, some for the first time, to choose our own way and to go forward with a lifestyle of real worship of the real God.

This is liberating!

And it is God's desire that you and I understand it!

The apostle Paul prayed for his readers about this.

> "I pray that from his glorious, unlimited resources he will empower you with inner strength through his Spirit. Then Christ will make his home in your hearts as you trust in him. Your roots will grow down into God's love and keep you strong. And may you have the power to understand, as all God's people should, how wide, how long, how high, and how deep his love is. May you experience the love of Christ, though it is too great to understand fully. Then you will be made complete with all the fullness of life and power that comes from God." (Ephesians 3:16–19)

He's praying that the readers would sink their roots deep into the love of God—the eternal, unchanging, dependable, and consistent love—and that as a result of this love of God, they would be made 'complete.'

Ultimately, that's what those who are bowing down at the idol of popularity are looking for: a consistent, accepting kind of love that liberates us from fear and allows us to be ourselves—our real, complete selves.

That is the love that that ninth-grade boy was looking for, and eventually *I* found it, after several years of desperate searching. (But you already knew that).

That is the love that the ninth-grade girl knew and a big part of the reason that *my wife* was such a positive influence on so many people, even at a young age.

That's the love that God has for us, and He wants us to experience it fully!

That's why Paul wrote,

> "What shall we say about such wonderful things as these? If God is for us, who can ever be against us? Since he did not spare even his own Son but gave him up for us all, won't he also give us everything else? Who dares accuse us whom God has chosen for his own? No one—for God himself has given us right standing with himself. Who then will condemn us? No one—for Christ Jesus died for us and was raised to life for us, and he is sitting in the place of honor at God's right hand, pleading for us.
>
> Can anything ever separate us from Christ's love? Does it mean he no longer loves us if we have trouble or calamity, or are persecuted, or hungry, or destitute, or in danger, or threatened with death? (As the Scriptures say, "For your sake we are killed every day; we are being slaughtered like sheep.") No, despite all

these things, overwhelming victory is ours through Christ, who loved us.

And I am convinced that nothing can ever separate us from God's love. Neither death nor life, neither angels nor demons, neither our fears for today nor our worries about tomorrow—not even the powers of hell can separate us from God's love. No power in the sky above or in the earth below—indeed, nothing in all creation will ever be able to separate us from the love of God that is revealed in Christ Jesus our Lord." (Romans 8:31–39)

God—the Creator of the universe—knows you and loves you!

Know His love! Accept His love! Rest in His love! Let His love free you up to be yourself, and go share it with others!

Then, and only then, will you be able to cast down the idol of popularity, to stop bowing to other people's opinions, and to become strong, free, and independent. Only by basing our lives on the 'rock' of Jesus and understanding God's love for us will we ever learn to be free.

We will stop believing the lies that we have to do something remarkable in order to be special or that we need to cave to the pressure others put on us to conform.

As the apostle Paul would rightly say,

"Therefore, I urge you, brothers and sisters, in view of God's mercy, to offer your bodies as a living sacrifice, holy and pleasing to God—this is your true and proper worship. Do not conform to the pattern of this world, but be transformed by the renewing of your mind. Then you will be able to test and approve what God's will is—his good, pleasing and perfect will." (Romans 12:1–2)

Only by rejecting the lies of this world's philosophies and building our lives on God's Word and His character will we ever have the strong foundation to live in secure freedom. Only by offering ourselves—all day, every day—to the Lord will we truly experience the exhilaration of knowing that He is working within us! Only then will we be able to "test and approve what God's will is," by following Him. And only then will we begin to fully realize that God's will for us isn't to ruin all our fun or to rain on our parade. Rather, God's will for us is 'good, pleasing and perfect'!

God's will for us is the best way to the best life!

That's part of what Jesus meant when He said that He had come so that His followers (not simply those who say they believe in Him but those who actually live that way) would have "Life ... to the Full" (John 10:10).

Our culture's acceptance is an ever-changing target with a faulty goal. If we make it our idol, we will be forever bowing down yet never actually finding acceptance. Instead, committing our way to the Lord and accepting what He says about us is the way to stability, health, and acceptance.

CHAPTER 5
THE IDOL OF SEX

COUNTERFEIT: IMITATION, FORGERY, UNREAL, FAKE

In the United States, between $70 million and $200 million of counterfeit money is in circulation. Inside the United States, the twenty-dollar bill is the most counterfeited in our economy. Abroad, it's the $100 dollar bill.

The United States Secret Service is responsible for anti-counterfeiting efforts within the US Treasury Department.

Before I went to college, I worked in a bank as a 'Teller'.

Ironically, it seemed to me, I was never instructed to spot counterfeit bills, per se. Instead, I was instructed how to spot—and to know the 'real thing'.

They reasoned that, if we could know the genuine, we would not be fooled by whatever tried to pass as counterfeit.

In their anti-counterfeiting efforts, the government uses special paper, die, watermarks, imprints, hairs, and other means to make it more and more difficult to make counterfeit bills that will be mistaken for the 'genuine article'.

Counterfeits—fakes and lies—cost everyone!

Counterfeiters try to pass off a fake as if they are the real thing; of course, they're only a cheap copy. In fact, they have no value—zero—because they are not backed by the government of the United States.

There is another counterfeit in our country, and this one may be even more destructive!

Remember that idea we started with: that Americans—and in particular, American Christians—are increasingly guilty of spiritual idolatry in lots of ways—one of the primary ones being worshipping at the altar of sexual indulgence.

Remember what we said about idolatry. It is worship, service, or devotion to something that is not God, as though it were God; giving God's rightful place of ultimate devotion to someone or something else.

In the first chapter of this book, we saw that the Israelites were guilty of idolatry and, specifically, of worshipping the god Baal. A big part of that was illicit sex—with religious prostitutes, with multiple partners, and even in groups. This was all part of the *worship* of the god Baal, which was, essentially, a 'god of the flesh'—a god of earthly things, a god of nature worship, revelry, sexual promiscuity, and the sacrifice of their children.

The God of the Hebrews was calling them out of that lifestyle and establishing Israel as a new nation—a nation through which He would reveal His will, His standards, and His plan for the world and, ultimately, His Son—the Way, Truth, and Life!

They were encouraged and warned to worship Him *only*, serve Him *only*, and obey Him *only!*

Exodus 20:1–5 says,

And God spoke all these words:

"I am the Lord your God, who brought you out of Egypt, out of the land of slavery. "You shall have no other gods before me. "You shall not make for yourself an image in the form of anything in heaven above or on the earth beneath or in the waters below. You shall not bow down to them or worship them …"

Do not copy the religious practices of the people around them. Do not compromise with the nations around them. Do not worship their 'gods.' Yet they did. Throughout the Old Testament, we see that Israel vacillated between honoring and worshipping God and idolatry.

Most times they committed idolatry, it involved sexual sin. Why? Because sexual sin is the most basic, self-centered sin there is. It starts in our basic instincts and selfish desires, and it stays there—*unless* God redeems us and thereby redeems it!

One of the most prominent ways that this "idolatry" shows in our culture is in the elevation of sex and sexual fulfillment above all reason. Sex sells, and it shows up in everything from television to fashion, magazines to pornography, to illicit and unbiblical relationships. Sexual imagery accounts for 20 percent of all advertisements, most notably in ads for alcohol, entertainment, and beauty products.[9], [10]

The bottom line, according to the philosophy of this world, is 'My sexual satisfaction is my right and no one—not even God—has the right to infringe on my sexual fulfillment!'

---

[9] https://www.businessnewsdaily.com/2649-sex-sells-more.html#:~:text=Advertisers%20use%20sexual%20imagery%20to,because%20it%20immediately%20grabs%20attention.

[10] *Journal of Current Issues and Research in Advertising.* Leonard Reid, a professor of advertising at UGA Grady College, and Courtney Carpenter Childers, an assistant professor in the School of Advertising and Public Relations at the University of Tennessee, Knoxville, are coauthors of the study.

This is obviously *way* out of line, but it has worked its way into our classrooms, our politics, and is infringing on biblically based truth. It has even infected our churches and is being taught from some pulpits! This is a great indicator that the *spirit of the age* has crept in, much as Baal worship did to the people of Israel.

Stubborn pride, which refuses to submit itself to God, is powerfully seen in the area of sexual behavior. This attitude—and the behaviors that go along with it—must be repented of before we can experience His blessing.

Our sexual sins, and our stubborn refusal to repent of them, is evidence of our internal uncleanness.

Jesus said it this way:

> "All of you listen," he said, "and try to understand. It's not what goes into your body that defiles you; you are defiled by what comes from your heart."
>
> Then Jesus went into a house to get away from the crowd, and his disciples asked him what he meant by the parable he had just used. "Don't you understand either?" he asked. "Can't you see that the food you put into your body cannot defile you? Food doesn't go into your heart, but only passes through the stomach and then goes into the sewer." (By saying this, he declared that every kind of food is acceptable in God's eyes.)
>
> And then he added, "It is what comes from inside that defiles you. For from within, out of a person's heart, come evil thoughts, sexual immorality, theft, murder, adultery, greed, wickedness, deceit, lustful desires, envy, slander, pride, and foolishness. All these vile things come from within; they are what defile you." (Mark 7:14–23)

Jesus said that it is in the heart that we are "defiled" because the heart that is not redeemed—the heart that is not changed by God—is essentially a self-centered, idolatrous heart.

Remember that Jeremiah 17:9 says, "The human heart is the most deceitful of all things, and desperately wicked."

Without the grace and work of God in our lives and our world, we will be self-centered. We will deceive ourselves to think right is wrong and wrong is right, and our self-interests will come out on top in almost every case.

It shows up in *many* ways. One of the most important is how it shows up in our sex and sexuality.

Remember how God first designed us.

> "Then the LORD God said, "It is not good for the man to be alone. I will make a helper who is just right for him." So the LORD God formed from the ground all the wild animals and all the birds of the sky. He brought them to the man to see what he would call them, and the man chose a name for each one. He gave names to all the livestock, all the birds of the sky, and all the wild animals. But still, there was no helper just right for him.
>
> So the LORD God caused the man to fall into a deep sleep. While the man slept, the LORD God took out one of the man's ribs and closed up the opening. Then the LORD God made a woman from the rib, and he brought her to the man.
>
> "At last!" the man exclaimed.
>
> "This one is bone from my bone,
> and flesh from my flesh!

> She will be called 'woman,'
> because she was taken from 'man.'"
>
> This explains why a man leaves his father and mother and is joined to his wife, and the two are united into one.
>
> Now the man and his wife were both naked, but they felt no shame." (Genesis 2:18–25)

Some look at this as simply *'descriptive'* and not *'prescriptive.'* In other words, the simple fact that God made male and female so that they would need each other to continue the race was simply the way it was. That doesn't mean that's the way it should be. I disagree. This is God's pattern seen throughout the natural world and all of known history.

Others argue that this is just the Old Testament; the New Testament writers didn't care.

Remember though that Jesus reaffirmed this design and taught its importance.

Matthew 19:4–6 says,

> "Haven't you read the Scriptures?" Jesus replied. "They record that from the beginning 'God made them male and female.'" And he said, "'This explains why a man leaves his father and mother and is joined to his wife, and the two are united into one. Since they are no longer two but one, let no one split apart what God has joined together."

God made them male and female to complement one another, to complete the natural *Image of God* within humankind, and to enable the continuation of the species.

Their relationship was to be one of openness, authenticity, freedom, and beauty—and that included their sexual relationship!

Sex within marriage—far from being something to be ashamed of or embarrassed about—is to be celebrated and enjoyed!

The Song of Solomon in the Bible has some of the most romantic language about the sexual relationship between a husband and wife there is, and it's beautiful.

And *God included it in His Word!*

That's because God designed sex in part for procreation, in part for intimacy, and in part for pleasure. But almost immediately after He put Adam and Eve into the garden, they sinned and went against God. And *everything* changed. Sin entered their hearts, and they realized they were naked and hid from God and each other.

And it's been happening ever since.

Their hearts were changed, and all of the world was changed. What theologians call *the fall of man* corrupted everything from nature to man's view of himself and his relationships with God and others.

The heart became self-centered (as opposed to God and other-centered). This has continued over the years and has impacted every area of our lives, certainly including sex and sexuality.

In our country, the so-called *sexual revolution* of the sixties promised no limits on sexual expression. Birth control made it so that, for the most part, people could have sex and not think about the natural outcome of doing so. But it didn't work.

The statistics bear this out.

- In the 1940s, the number of out-of-wedlock births in the USA was somewhere between 2 percent and 3 percent.
- In the 1950s, the same number held true.

- In the 1960s, the figure jumped to 5 percent—a disturbing trend but not a huge number.
- By 1980, that number had jumped to 18.4 percent.
- And in 2020, the percentage of children born out of wedlock was 40 percent![11]

This was all *after* birth control became easily and readily available. In fact, in 1940, there was almost no birth control available. Today, it's not only available, but in some cases, it's supplied for free by the schools!

Statistically, with those numbers, I think we can say clearly that the sexual revolution was a failure!

Sex, rather than part of the beautiful relationship of the man and the woman in the garden, became "all about me!" "If *you* can make *me* feel good, then that's all that it's about."

In our desire—our *insistence* and stubbornness, our *idolatry* of sex—we have convinced ourselves that we are living free, yet in truth, we are more enslaved than ever.

Take pornography, for example.

Some think of porn as a victimless vice. In their minds, the user is not hurting anyone, so what is the harm?

Pornography

Americans spend $10 billion annually on various forms of porn.

Approximately 200,000 Americans can be classified as "porn addicts."[12]

---

[11] https://www.cdc.gov/nchs/data/databriefs/db18.pdf
https://www.cdc.gov/nchs/fastats/unmarried-childbearing.htm.
[12] https://www.webroot.com/us/en/resources/tips-articles/internet-pornography-by-the-numbers#:~:text=About%20200%2C000%20Americans%20are%20classified,ads%2C%20misdirected%20links%20or%20emails.

Five out of every ten men *in church* are struggling with pornography. Many more men outside the church utilize it also. One out of every six women grapples with addiction to pornography. Porn grabs a hold of a person and won't let go. It predominantly affects men but also women, especially when you include fantasy novels and so-called *mommy porn* like *Fifty Shades of Grey*.

As it does so, it tears apart the bond of the husband to the wife and vice versa. It entices the user to escape into fantasy with increasing frequency. It forces the actual partner to compete with a produced, fake, counterfeit partner who never has a bad day, never gains weight, never has muscles that turn flabby, and never stops performing.

Against this counterfeit, the genuine, actual, real spouse cannot compete. Marriages are damaged, and often destroyed, all in the name of *self-satisfaction*. Pornography, far from being harmless, is insidious and profoundly harmful.

Pornography is not the only way that sex has become an idol.

Sex before Marriage

Societal attitudes regarding premarital sex have changed dramatically over the last few decades. In one study, the percentage of those who said this was 'not wrong at all' went from about 27 percent in 1975 to about 65 percent in 2018!

In 2019, the CDC says that 38 percent of teens say they have been sexually active.[13]

That means, of course, that roughly 60 percent have *not* been!

When people become sexually intimate before marriage, they open themselves up to sexually transmitted diseases, pregnancy, and emotional pain.

---

[13] https://www.cdc.gov/healthyyouth/data/yrbs/feature/index.htm.

For those who are able to avoid STDs and pregnancy and claim to have zero emotional pain, they are opening themselves up to a coarsening of their hearts.

It's sort of like developing a callous.

If you have repeated exposure of your skin to an irritant that rubs against it, you will often develop very painful blisters. If you continue doing that activity in spite of the pain and blistering, eventually you will develop a callous.

At times, this can be a good thing—when you're learning to play the bass guitar, for example. However, developing "callouses" on our hearts is never a good thing! Yet that's precisely what happens when we have multiple sexual partners. Our hearts, which are designed for emotional and sexual intimacy, become irritated then 'blister' with pain. If we stop, they can heal. If we continue, however, we will develop emotional and sexual 'callouses.'

This will impede our relationships, once we do decide to settle down and enter a committed relationship. The more sexual partners you have before marriage, the more likely you are to struggle with sexual temptation *in* your marriage.

Some may retort, "I don't have multiple sexual partners before marriage, only one, so what's the harm?" Statistically, however, those who live together before marriage are far less likely to follow through and get married. Those who are sexually active before marriage are more likely to break up before marriage or to divorce after they marry.

Conversely, of those who report that they've waited together to have sex until after marriage, 72 percent report being 'very satisfied' with their sexual relationship—more than 40 percent higher than those who were *not* committed to waiting![14]

---

[14] https://www.theatlantic.com/health/archive/2018/10/sexual-partners-and-marital-happiness/573493/.

Adultery

Adultery—the biblical term for being sexually active with someone other than your spouse—is devastating to a marriage. It wrecks marriages, destroys families, and obliterates relationships. Yet statistically, 30 to 60 percent of those married in the US commit adultery at some time in their lives, and it is increasingly common for couples under the age of thirty.[15]

Men are more likely to commit adultery than women, but that is leveling out as the 'sexual revolution' poisons more women too.

About one quarter of all divorces happen due to adultery. When we add *emotional adultery*, in which two people share intimate secrets with one another and develop a secretly intimate emotional relationship with someone other than their spouse, it is even more devastating. Additionally, *virtual adultery*, in which two people who are not married act out sexually with one another—from a distance, via online media—is also devastating to relationships and can lead to in-person physical adultery.

These are all increasingly common with the advent of social media sites and with the increasing use of instant messaging apps.

It is possible, now more than ever, to be sexually and emotionally involved with someone other than your spouse, giving attention, communication, and intimate details that should only be shared with our husband or wife. One thing is certain: as virtual technology becomes more easily used, and of higher quality and resolution, this trend will not only continue but probably increase!

Masturbation

Not directly dealt with in the Bible, this is dealt with in principle.

---

[15] https://comparecamp.com/cheating-statistics/.

Today, many experts speak of masturbation as normal and healthy and something that should be assumed and normalized.[16] They say that it's a healthy way to deal with one's sexual urges without acting them out and thereby causing more problems (some of which are mentioned in this chapter).

From one perspective, I think it needs to be said that this is true. It may be better to act out alone, in your own fantasy world, than to do so in reality, thereby exposing ourselves and others to pregnancy, disease, and emotional and sexual pain. However, from a biblical perspective, it is still wrong, and here's why: Masturbation is always associated with lust. It is one person acting out on that person's urges. It is me giving in to my own cravings for sexual fulfillment. Masturbation is often (but not always) coupled with pornography or fantasy, which is viewed as sin in the scriptures.

It virtually always makes sex a completely self-centered activity devoid of relationship, which is not God's original design. Additionally, masturbation can be highly addictive, leading to problems in actual relationships. Through masturbation, we reach climax and orgasm, which releases so-called *pleasure hormones* in our brain—without the complications associated with actual relationships. This can be increasingly enticing, and difficult to stop, once an actual relationship is commenced.

Just so we're clear, masturbation affects men and women.

If I am into a habit of fantasy and masturbation, I am setting up any present or future *real* relationships for unrealistic expectations and failure.

---

[16] https://jamanetwork.com/journals/jamapediatrics/fullarticle/1107656.

Homosexuality

Approximately 4 to 5 percent of the population consider themselves 'homosexual'—that is, committed to this as a lifestyle in which one seeks sexual intimacy and fulfillment with someone of one's same sex. The percentage has increased over the past ten years.[17]

Approximately 65 percent of Americans view it as *morally neutral* and should be accepted, while 35 percent view it as morally wrong.[18] Several churches and denominations have, over the past decade, sought to "normalize" and legitimize homosexuality, from the Word of God's perspective.

In my view, this is not legitimate. Rather than get into each individual passage and the arguments for and against homosexuality, I'd rather take a big-picture approach.

In the Bible, homosexuality is *never* mentioned positively in the scripture—*always* associated with sin. Jesus never specifically mentioned it, but He *did* reaffirm the 'one man, one woman, male and female, *becoming one*' pattern God had designed, as already mentioned (Matthew 19:4–6).

Several Bible passages have recently been reinterpreted to make homosexuality more palatable but still cannot change the original design and procreation purposes. Other passages are simply ignored. Some scriptures, judged by today's cultural standards as 'too narrow-minded,' are rejected.

Romans 1:24–27 says,

> "Therefore God gave them over in the sinful desires
> of their hearts to sexual impurity for the degrading

---

[17] https://www.statista.com/statistics/719674/american-adults-who-identify-as-homosexual-bisexual-or-transgender/.

[18] https://www.statista.com/statistics/225968/americans-moral-stance-towards-gay-or-lesbian-relations/.

of their bodies with one another. They exchanged the truth about God for a lie, and worshiped and served created things rather than the Creator—who is forever praised. Amen.

Because of this, God gave them over to shameful lusts. Even their women exchanged natural sexual relations for unnatural ones. In the same way the men also abandoned natural relations with women and were inflamed with lust for one another. Men committed shameful acts with other men, and received in themselves the due penalty for their error."

The scriptures are clear that we do not have the right to pick and choose—cafeteria style—from the portions of scripture we like and reject those we don't like. As the scriptures themselves testify, "All Scripture is God-breathed and is useful for teaching, rebuking, correcting and training in righteousness" (2 Timothy 3:16). See also Psalm 1, 19:1–4; Isaiah 40; 1 Peter 1:24.

I do believe it's important to point out that there is a difference between *same-sex attraction* and those who act out homosexually. Struggling with same-sex attraction is, in many ways, like struggling with any other kind of sexual temptation. Abstinence *can* be achieved, and victory over temptation can be received!

The church must love people who struggle with this and invite them into our fellowship so that they may—as we all need to—overcome and walk in the blessing of God!

It is true churches have historically done a poor job admitting the reality of these temptations and welcoming those who struggle with them into their fellowship. It would be better to correct course now than to continue on a faulty and biblically idolatrous path! In any of these sexual temptations, we need to welcome people in, allow them to admit their struggles, and walk with them into victory and holiness.

Transgenderism

While whole books can and should be written about this issue, for our purposes, I must be brief. Gender confusion and gender identity are concepts that have gone from 'fringe' ideas to 'mainstream' at breakneck speed! Young children are declaring that they are identifying as the opposite gender than their biological reality, and well-meaning parents and professionals are affirming this. Hormone blockers, sex reassignment surgery, and 'gender-affirming pronouns' are increasingly common.

According to an article in Women's Health Magazine (https://www.womenshealthmag.com/relationships/a36395721/gender-identity-list/) there are at least 16 separate ways of understanding gender...and all are equally valid and healthy. While Christ-followers should love and affirm the people dealing with this confusion, we can still come back to God's original design as our guide. People who are confused and struggling to identify with the sex that God assigned to them at birth should be helped, counseled, and loved—but ultimately, directed to accept God's will for them, which is His design. Rather than changing definitions and the reality that has been accepted from time immemorial, we should reaffirm the obvious male/female order of creation, and help our friends to adjust more fully.

We do *not* want to communicate that these issues are 'no big deal', that God doesn't care, nor do we want to communicate that they are beyond the love, grace, and power of God or that they are beyond the loving embrace of the church.

A big part of the problem is that our culture has separated itself from the way God wanted to work in our lives. Over the last several decades, we have increasingly pushed God out of the public square and revelled—as a culture—in our independence and freedom. We've convinced ourselves as a culture that unlimited sexual expression—what we could call sexual freedom—is a good thing.

But that's not how it was designed, and in truth, we're deceiving ourselves.

The *big* problem is this: the church has bought into this mindset as well! Some of us who claim to be Christ followers have been more influenced by our society than by the Word of God on this, and that's bad.

First Corinthians 6:9–11 says,

> Don't you realize that those who do wrong will not inherit the Kingdom of God? Don't fool yourselves. Those who indulge in sexual sin, or who worship idols, or commit adultery, or are male prostitutes, or practice homosexuality, or are thieves, or greedy people, or drunkards, or are abusive, or cheat people—none of these will inherit the Kingdom of God. Some of you were once like that. But you were cleansed; you were made holy; you were made right with God by calling on the name of the Lord Jesus Christ and by the Spirit of our God."

Paul, along with the other writers of the New Testament, speaks as though *there should be a change* in the life, attitude, and behavior of the Christ follower! I may have been all about drunkenness, partying, greediness, and various kinds of sexual sin before, *but I should not continue to be* if I've come to Christ.

> "You say, "I am allowed to do anything"—but not everything is good for you. And even though "I am allowed to do anything," I must not become a slave to anything." (v.12)

In context, in the community of Corinth, some were teaching that *since God forgives all sin, it did not matter how they behaved*. In fact, they could revel in their freedom because of grace. They were so into reveling in their freedom that their freedom was leading to enslavement again, like so many of us feel when it comes to our 'sexual freedom.' What seemed to start out with the promise of freedom has led, in fact, to our enslavement.

> "You say, "Food was made for the stomach, and the stomach for food. This is true, though someday God will do away with both of them." (v. 13)

They're saying, in essence, 'It's just nature. It's natural to eat and shouldn't be limited, in the same way, we should be allowed to do what comes naturally with our bodies; it's a natural instinct.'

> "But you can't say that our bodies were made for sexual immorality. They were made for the Lord, and the Lord cares about our bodies. And God will raise us from the dead by his power, just as he raised our Lord from the dead.
>
> Don't you realize that your bodies are actually parts of Christ? Should a man take his body, which is part of Christ, and join it to a prostitute? Never! And don't you realize that if a man joins himself to a prostitute, he becomes one body with her? For the Scriptures say, "The two are united into one." But the person who is joined to the Lord is one spirit with him." (vv.13-17)

Paul is teaching that, when a person comes to Jesus Christ, they become *one* with Him. In a sense, everywhere that person goes, everything that person does—everything—Jesus is part of. If I allow myself to commit sexual sin, I am bringing Him into it also, and as a Christian, I have no right to do so! Paul says that instead of insisting on our "rights" to our sexual sins and stubbornly presuming on the grace of God, we should instead handle it this way:

> "Run from sexual sin! No other sin so clearly affects the body as this one does. For sexual immorality is a sin against your own body. Don't you realize that your body is the temple of the Holy Spirit, who lives in you and was given to you by God? You do not belong to yourself, for God bought you with a high price. So you must honor God with your body." (vv.18-20)

God calls us who are Christ followers to rise above all these sexual sins things that our world wants to revel in—as well as the other sins mentioned.

Ironically, in our insistence on sexual freedom, more and more people have become enslaved to sexual practices that are increasingly harmful, costly, and further and further away from God's beautiful picture of one man and one woman in a committed, lifelong, loving relationship.

All of these sins are equally powerful within us, because sex was designed to be much more than a biological or physiological function.

In the human being—made in the image of God—sex has a 'oneness' aspect to it, and when you have sex—no matter who it's with—you *become one* with them to a degree. And this is only designed by the Creator to happen within a committed, one-man-one-woman, married, and lifelong relationship.

A Better Way

So instead of letting our *culture* define us, sexually, we need to let God, His Word, and the Holy Spirit define us and, in some cases, redefine us.

"So I say, let the Holy Spirit guide your lives. Then you won't be doing what your sinful nature craves. The sinful nature wants to do evil, which is just the opposite of what the Spirit wants. And the Spirit gives us desires that are the opposite of what the sinful nature desires. These two forces are constantly fighting each other, so you are not free to carry out your good intentions. But when you are directed by the Spirit, you are not under obligation to the law of Moses.

When you follow the desires of your sinful nature, the results are very clear: sexual immorality, impurity, lustful pleasures, idolatry, sorcery, hostility, quarreling, jealousy, outbursts of anger, selfish ambition, dissension, division, envy, drunkenness, wild parties, and other sins like these. Let me tell you again, as I have before, that anyone living that sort of life will not inherit the Kingdom of God.

But the Holy Spirit produces this kind of fruit in our lives: love, joy, peace, patience, kindness, goodness, faithfulness, gentleness, and self-control. There is no law against these things!

Those who belong to Christ Jesus have nailed the passions and desires of their sinful nature to his cross and crucified them there. Since we are living by the Spirit, let us follow the Spirit's leading in every part of our lives." (Galatians 5:16–25)

What the church—and individual Christians—should do *instead* of giving in and adopting the unbiblical standards of our culture is to accept and encourage each other to admit our struggles in this area and to look to the Lord for victory over these temptations and sins.

These things may not be important to our culture. Our culture says we're archaic and old-fashioned, narrow-minded, and even judgmental. But we must answer to God and His Word, not our culture, and His Word makes it pretty clear what His desire is.

> "Finally, dear brothers and sisters, we urge you in the name of the Lord Jesus to live in a way that pleases God, as we have taught you. You live this way already, and we encourage you to do so even more. For you remember what we taught you by the authority of the Lord Jesus.
>
> God's will is for you to be holy, so stay away from all sexual sin. Then each of you will control his own body and live in holiness and honor—not in lustful passion like the pagans who do not know God and his ways.
>
> Never harm or cheat a Christian brother in this matter by violating his wife, for the Lord avenges all such sins, as we have solemnly warned you before. God has called us to live holy lives, not impure lives. Therefore, anyone who refuses to live by these rules is not disobeying human teaching but is rejecting God, who gives his Holy Spirit to you." (1 Thessalonians 4:1–8)

'Stay away from all sexual sin,' and control your own body, living in holiness and honor.

We need to call it what it is.

If our sexual temptations and sexual behaviors are outside the revealed will and design of God—that is, one man and one woman in a lifelong, committed relationship of marriage—then they are sin and should be treated as such. That is, they should be acknowledged, confessed, repented of, and left behind.

Those who struggle with these sexual sins—*any of them*—should be loved, accepted, encouraged, helped, and held accountable.

Sex and sexuality are one part of who we are, but it's not *all* we are. It's a big part of our identity, but not *all* of our identity.

Remember that idolatry is giving God's rightful place of worship, obedience, and attention to someone or something that doesn't rightfully observe it. In our culture, sex and sexuality have taken God's rightful place in many lives. We want to push back on that and make sure that philosophy isn't infiltrating the church. Why?

Because we want to always give God His rightful place in our lives and because we know that acknowledging Him, submitting to Him, following Him, and worshipping Him is the best way to live.

"Jesus said, 'The thief comes only to steal, kill, and destroy; I have come that they might have LIFE and have it To The Full!" (John 10:10, emphasis mine.). We've allowed Satan—the deceiver, the liar, and thief—to steal our sexuality away from us. We need to take it back and give it back to God, letting Him define and refine us.

I'd like to ask you to honestly reflect, please. If you need to admit before God that you've compromised your standards on this issue of sex and sexuality, confess that to God.

If you have to admit that you've been a bit stubborn and have willingly bought our culture's lies about this part of your life, admit that to God. If you'd like to ask God's forgiveness in this area, stop right where you are and speak it out to God. If you're ready to let God define you, redefine you, and give you a new standard, a new heart, and a new and fresh start sexually, tell Him so!

Now let me encourage you to do one more thing. If you're serious about what you just talked to God about, *please* tell a believer you trust!

Seek their prayers, encouragement, and accountability. Don't allow your spiritual enemy, Satan—the liar and deceiver—to convince you to keep it to yourself. The dark corners of our heart and mind are where he does his most destructive work. If we allow the light of truth to shine there, his power is greatly reduced! Fear and shame are two of his most effective tools, but if you confess these struggles to a trusted Christian friend or pastor, fear and shame are eliminated.

First John 4:18 says, "There is no fear in love. But perfect love drives out fear."

Perhaps it's time you allowed God's perfect love for you—as shown in the perfect, complete work of Jesus Christ on your behalf—to drive out the fear and shame within and thus to disarm your spiritual accuser and enemy!

CHAPTER 6
THE IDOL OF AMERICA!

NO, THAT IS NOT A MISTAKE.

I believe that America itself can be (and has become) an idol for some Americans.

American values, *American-made* products, American exceptionalism, American government, American traditions—all of these things can become idols if looked at the wrong way.

Let's remember our working definition of the word *idolatry*. It means worship, service, or devotion to something that is not God, as though it were God; giving God's rightful place of ultimate devotion to someone or something else.

'Whoa!' you might say. 'I get that it *can* be a problem, but America is a Christian nation! How can that be an idol'?

I would certainly agree that America started as a nation that was very friendly to the Judeo-Christian tradition and the God of the Bible.

America was founded as a representative republic. It was founded this way to ensure freedom from tyranny, and much of the motivation for that came from a desire to escape religious persecution in the old country. The Pilgrims came to America in search of a new opportunity—most notably to worship the Lord as they saw fit and not as the Church of England saw fit.

William Bradford and the *Mayflower* settlers crafted a document that was filled with Christian principles: the Mayflower Compact. It started with these words:

> "IN THE NAME OF GOD, AMEN. We, whose names are underwritten, the Loyal Subjects of our dread Sovereign Lord King *James*, by the Grace of God, of *Great Britain*, *France*, and *Ireland*, King, *Defender of the Faith*, &c. Having undertaken for the Glory of God, and Advancement of the Christian Faith, and the Honour of our King and Country, a Voyage to plant the first Colony in the northern Parts of *Virginia*; Do by these Presents, solemnly and mutually, in the Presence of God and one another, covenant and combine ourselves together into a civil Body Politick …"[19]

They were very definitely submitted to God and each other as they tried to advance the Gospel in this new land.

This compact, which was signed by all, formed the basis for many of our laws and government.

Later, pilgrims would come from Great Britain to escape the religious tyranny of the Church of England and the power of the king to infringe on their worship. They knew that the God of the Bible—and their Christian faith—was instrumental in this endeavor.

---

[19] Peter Marshall and David Manuel, *The Light and the Glory*, 120.

John Winthrop, one of the founders of the Massachusetts Bay Colony, said to the people he was leading into this new world,

> "Beloved there is now set before us life, and good, death and evil in that we are Commanded this day to love the Lord our God, and to love one another to walk in his ways and to keep his Commandments and his Ordinance, and his laws, and the Articles of our Covenant with him that we may live and be multiplied, and that the Lord our God may bless us in the land whether we go to possess it:
>
> But if our hearts shall turn away so that we will not obey, but shall be seduced and worship other Gods our pleasures, and profits, and serve them, it is propounded unto us this day, we shall surely perish out of the good Land whether we pass over this vast Sea to possess it."[20]

Yet it would not keep them submitted to the home country, as the Founders about 150 years later would declare,

> "When in the Course of human events, it becomes necessary for one people to dissolve the political bands which have connected them with another, and to assume among the powers of the earth, the separate and equal station to which the Laws of Nature and of Nature's God entitle them, a decent respect to the opinions of mankind requires that they should declare the causes which impel them to the separation."

---

[20] Ibid, p. 162.

And what were their reasons?

> "We hold these truths to be self-evident, that all men are created equal, that they are endowed by their Creator with certain unalienable Rights, that among these are Life, Liberty and the pursuit of Happiness.— That to secure these rights, Governments are instituted among Men, deriving their just powers from the consent of the governed,—That whenever any Form of Government becomes destructive of these ends, it is the Right of the People to alter or to abolish it, and to institute new Government, laying its foundation on such principles and organizing its powers in such form, as to them shall seem most likely to effect their Safety and Happiness."[20]

For Americans, this was a *great* day, and we look back every year to celebrate that Declaration of Independence on July 4.

Many of us also celebrate the fact that so many of the Founders embraced Christianity as part of their reasoning.

George Washington said,

> "It is the duty of all nations to acknowledge the providence of Almighty God, to obey His will, to be grateful for His benefits, and humbly to implore His protection and favor."[21]

---

[21] Washington's Thanksgiving Declaration, October 3, 1789.

He also said,

> "Of all the dispositions and habits which lead to political prosperity, religion and morality are indispensable."[22]

Thomas Jefferson said,

> "God who gave us life gave us liberty. Can the liberties of a nation be thought secure when we have removed their only firm basis—a conviction in the minds of the people that these liberties are of the Gift of God? That they are not to be violated but with His wrath? Indeed, I tremble for my country when I reflect that God is just; that His justice cannot sleep forever."[23]

Patrick Henry said,

> "It cannot be emphasized too strongly or too often that this great nation was founded, not by religionists, but by Christians; not on religions, but on the gospel of Jesus Christ. For this very reason peoples of other faiths have been afforded asylum, prosperity, and freedom of worship here."[24]

Yet the laws and government policies were not enough. John Adams said,

> "We have no government armed with power capable of contending with human passions unbridled by morality and religion. Avarice, ambition, revenge,

---

[22] Washington's Farewell Address, September 17, 1796, via wikisource.
[23] Notes on the State of Virginia, Query XVIII, 237.
[24] *The Trumpet Voice of Freedom: Patrick Henry of Virginia*, iii.

or gallantry would break the strongest cords of our Constitution as a whale goes through a net.

Our Constitution was made only for a moral and religious people. It is wholly inadequate to the government of any other."[25]

Make no mistake: The United States of America very definitely started as a Christian nation. The principles it was founded on were very much centered around a God-centered vision.

The Constitution itself was framed to limit the power of the government and its ability to infringe on individual freedom.

Today, most would admit that the country that is America has definitely changed.

While many Christians would call us back to those principles, many more Americans would probably say they are *old-fashioned* or even *archaic*.

So is America still the best nation on earth?

Lest you think that America cannot be an idol, let me ask you these questions:

- Are there things that America stands for today that are unbiblical?
- Are there traditions that have become valued—even (dare I say it?) 'worshipped'—in our country today that might be outside the realm of biblical teachings?
- Are there instances where it seems impossible to separate our Christian faith from our American heritage?

---

[25] Letter to the Officers of the First Brigade of the Third Division of the Militia of Massachusetts, October 11, 1798, in Revolutionary Services and Civil Life of General William Hull.

I would certainly agree with many that the values that define America have changed. In many cases, they have become unbiblical.

Let's look at a couple of cultural expressions that have become big in America. I mean *big!*

Think of the celebrations of our holidays. New Year's Day, Valentine's Day, Easter, Memorial Day, Independence Day, Labor Day, Halloween, Thanksgiving Day, and Christmas Day are huge in America. The National Retail Federation has calculated that Americans spent a total of $789.4 *billion* in 2020 on the holidays between Thanksgiving and Christmas alone—despite the COVID pandemic![26]

Is that "kingdom of God" thinking? Is that putting God first over our lifestyle—much of which is tied up in "patriotic" traditions? No, it is *not!*

Jesus said,

> "Do not store up for yourselves treasures on earth, where moths and vermin destroy, and where thieves break in and steal. But store up for yourselves treasures in heaven, where moths and vermin do not destroy, and where thieves do not break in and steal. For where your treasure is, there your heart will be also." (Matthew 6:19–21)

In the book of Isaiah, we read,

> "Surely the nations are like a drop in a bucket;
> they are regarded as dust on the scales;
> he weighs the islands as though they were fine dust.
> Lebanon is not sufficient for altar fires,
> nor its animals enough for burnt offerings.

---

[26] https://nrf.com/media-center/press-releases.

Before him all the nations are as nothing;
they are regarded by him as worthless
and less than nothing.

With whom, then, will you compare God?
To what image will you liken him?
As for an idol, a metalworker casts it,
and a goldsmith overlays it with gold
and fashions silver chains for it.
A person too poor to present such an offering
selects wood that will not rot;
they look for a skilled worker
to set up an idol that will not topple.

Do you not know?
Have you not heard?
Has it not been told you from the beginning?
Have you not understood since the earth was founded?
He sits enthroned above the circle of the earth,
and its people are like grasshoppers.
He stretches out the heavens like a canopy,
and spreads them out like a tent to live in.

He brings princes to naught
and reduces the rulers of this world to nothing.
No sooner are they planted,
no sooner are they sown,
no sooner do they take root in the ground,
than he blows on them and they wither,
and a whirlwind sweeps them away like chaff.

"To whom will you compare me?
Or who is my equal?" says the Holy One.

Lift up your eyes and look to the heavens:
Who created all these?
He who brings out the starry host one by one
and calls forth each of them by name.
Because of his great power and mighty strength,
not one of them is missing." (Isaiah 40:15–26)

Against that backdrop, how can we Christians justify the amount of time, money, and energy we put into the traditions of this earth and in particular the "American" lifestyle?

If Christians—in America or anywhere else—are going to live according to the kingdom of God and kingdom principles, we must realize that the pursuits of our earthly existence—including the pride we take in being Americans—must fade and the emphasis on the kingdom of God must take center stage!

Think of it this way: America is 'the land of the free and home of the brave.' Our liberties are a blessing, to be sure. The freedoms of the press, and the freedom to assemble, worship are amazing. They are spelled out in the First Amendment to our Constitution.

However, if in some magical way we were able to get *every* nation on earth to be just like us, so that *every* citizen of the world was living under the same conditions we are, what would be the outcome?

Would they be blessed by that freedom? Yes! Would some of them be freed from oppression and tyranny? Yes!

And that would be wonderful.

But would any of them in this way come to Christ? Would any of them have an *eternal* change, just because they are free?

No.

Now some would object that because of freedom, and because that freedom is so biblical, it would be probable that some would come to Jesus, and that *may* be true, but not *necessarily* so. It is certainly not inevitable. Otherwise, we would not have the millions of Americans today who reject the Lord outright.

In other words, even if *every* person on earth became an American to the fullest extent, if that's where they stopped, they would still be eternally separated from God!

They would enjoy this life, to be sure, but as Christians, our goal should not be simply to enjoy this life and encourage others to do so. Rather, our goal should be to glorify God with our lives and encourage others to come to know Him and glorify Him also.

We need to start thinking differently, and that's why I believe that patriotism—even in America—can very definitely be an idol!

I personally am a very "patriotic" American, and I refuse to give in to the secularization of our country. I believe, however, that our ultimate hope is *not* in politicians, laws, or the US Supreme Court. Our ultimate hope is, and *must always be*, in the Lord Jesus Christ.

When we forget that and focus on our earthly country—even one as great as America—we have missed the mark and may have been duped by the enemy.

That is why I believe that the best thing that God-loving Americans can do for our country is to seek revival in our churches, starting with our own hearts. If God gets a hold of *us* first, then He'll spread His impact through us. We will boldly, passionately, and confidently seek to honor Him and spread His Word and His love in Jesus's name, and others will be saved.

That is our nation's best hope!

God wants to bless his children. In the New Testament, Jesus and the apostles make clear that, by faith in Jesus, we are adopted into God's family. Therefore, He wants to hear our prayers and act on our behalf.

I do not believe that this means he will heal our land as a political entity per se. I do believe that, as His children seek His face and turn from our compromise and idolatry, He will forgive us, and He will move in a big way. As we band together in America to do that, His blessing will come on His children. As we get the Gospel of Jesus out with greater urgency, He will move even more.

I do not know God's "big picture" plan for America. However, I do know that the church in America—God's children, through faith in Jesus Christ—must repent of our focus on being *great Americans* and concentrate instead on being *faithful Christians*. Then God will be pleased.

Ironically, because of the way our faith impacts our behavior, it is then—and only then—that we will be the *best* Americans.

It involves humility, repentance, and lifestyle change.

Are you ready?

CHAPTER 7
THE IDOL OF COMFORT

JUST IMAGINE A SUNNY DAY, TEMPERATURE ABOUT EIGHTY, AND A very slight breeze.

You're lying on your hammock on your back deck. The birds are singing, you've got a cool drink next to you, and you don't have a care in the world. You're feeling so relaxed that you doze off, and it's fine!

Is that how you would picture your most comfortable moment?

For some, it'd be different. It might involve being out on a boat fishing, lying on the beach, having a picnic in the park, or sitting on your front porch and watching the neighbors.

Each one of these things can be a nice "time-out" or a well-earned break. But as is often the case with our pleasures, they can change; they morph from a nice "treat" to an expectation or even a demand!

They become our idols.

For example, after I mow my lawn, I like to sit and drink a glass of ice water. I really enjoy doing so on my back patio, under the umbrella at our table, while listening to the birds.

It's nice, It's morally neutral, it can even be a blessing.

However, if I come to the point where I think I *deserve* it and *demand* it, then it is in danger of becoming an idol to me. If my wife or kids come out to me to talk during this relaxation time, or if they need me to cut it short—to go to the store or something—what will my reaction be?

If I get irritable, angry, or lash out, there's a good bet that my relaxation time has become an "idol" to me. I have placed the priority of comfort in the rightful place of my family.

Americans in general are prone to this.

In American culture, we are taught that we *deserve a break* today. We have every right to take it easy and to pursue *the good life*. That includes an almost insatiable desire for ease and comfort. From the cushy furniture we sit on to the beds we sleep in, comfortable living products are a multimillion-dollar industry in our culture.

Now don't get me wrong. I'm not saying that we should only sit on hard benches or sleep on rocks, simply that our pursuit of comfort leads us to sacrifice what is really important for what is *nice* but not necessary.

Sometimes it means we break the bank in order to purchase that new mattress set. I actually heard a commercial today for five-year payment plans on mattresses!

Maybe we overspend our budget to buy that new pool. Maybe it's simply that we get frustrated with our kids who want to play 'I am in my *comfort* time!', we think.

So you say, "I get it. Comfort may be a slight problem in our priorities, but an 'idol'?" Perhaps you think I'm overstating the case.

Remember our working definition of idolatry: worship, service, or devotion to something that is not God, as though it were God; giving God's rightful place of ultimate devotion to someone or something else.

Can you see how this fixation on comfort might become an idol and might stand in the way of God's rightful place? No?

me put it to you this way: On Sundays in the wintertime, do you stay in bed or at home (because it's too cold) rather than going to church with any regularity? In the springtime, when it's yard project time, do you skip church or church functions because it's just too nice? In the summertime, when school's out, do you stay home from church or church functions because it's too hot or because you want to get ready for the beach?

If so, then—at least on those occasions—you're putting *comfort and ease* before God.

"I object!" you say. "I can be a Christian wherever I'm at—even if I never go to church!" True. Technically, I can see that point. Biblically and practically, not so much.

> "Let us think of ways to motivate one another to acts of love and good works. And let us not neglect our meeting together, as some people do, but encourage one another, especially now that the day of his return is drawing near." (Hebrews 10:24–25)

The one-another and each-other phrases in the New Testament all speak of Christians in relationship with one another.

- "Love one another as I have loved you" (John 13:34).
- "All men will know that you are my disciples by your love for one another" (John 13:35).
- "Be kind and compassionate; tender-hearted, forgiving each other just as, in Christ, God has forgiven you" (Ephesians 4:32).
- "Serve one another in love" (Galatians 5:13).
- "Submit to one another, out of reverence for Christ" (Ephesians 5:21).

And on it goes!

No fewer than thirty-five times (according to the NIV) we are instructed in *one-another* language in the New Testament, as a way of living out the faith that we claim.

When you add the *each-other* commands, there are at least thirty more times that the Lord and the church leaders instruct, encourage, and command us to treat each other in ways that reflect our new spiritual life.

You and I—as followers of Christ—simply can't function at the level He would like us to as *independent Christians*. In fact, I think the testimony of the scripture is so strong in this regard that, *if* someone fancies himself as totally independent, there's a good bet he's not a Christian—at least not a growing one!

Can you have faith in Jesus while alone and isolated? Perhaps…but *should* you? Absolutely not!

Therefore, when you and I elect the comfort of our beds, our slippers, and our front porch with the newspaper and coffee instead of church, we are choosing comfort before God.

And it doesn't stop there.

Think about *serving* in your church. Do you participate on a serving team regularly?

Remember the scriptures teach that each of us is given at least one spiritual gift at the point of our salvation. That gift is not for us to hide away but to use—for God's glory and the church's good.

> "There are different kinds of gifts, but the same Spirit. There are different kinds of service, but the same Lord. There are different kinds of working, but the same God works all of them in all men. Now to each one the manifestation of the Spirit is given for the common good." (1 Corinthians 12:4–7)

If you want to read more about spiritual gifts and how they are meant to help the church, you can read 1 Corinthians 12-14; Ephesians 4:1-13; and Romans 12:1-8.

Think of it this way: you—the individual Christ follower—are totally unique. No one else has had your exact experiences. No one else has your exact personality. No one else has the same background as you (your family, your school, work, etc.). No one else has your exact same passions and drives. And no one else has the exact mix of all of these plus the gifts of the Holy Spirit working within in exactly the same way you do!

What is the point?

Simply this: *You* are crucial to the mission of the church! God has supernaturally gifted *you* for an important role within the church!

This is, quite frankly, not about *you!*

It is about the glory of God and the work of His people. It is about the role that the church—His body—plays in getting the Word about Jesus out and helping others to come to a growing faith in Christ.

And *you* have a role to play in that!

Can you *only* play that role or use that gift in church? No! You can use those spiritual gifts everywhere you go! But He *does* want you to use these gifts in church too!

That might mean getting out of your comfort zone. It might mean humbling yourself enough to do what He has gifted you to do—even if it's in virtual anonymity. On the other hand, it might mean standing up in front of the entire church to give your testimony—all to the glory of God.

Again, our comfort zone isn't the main concern. It's *not* about us! It is about the Lord, His glory, and our part to play in bringing Him *more* glory!

Some of you might be thinking, *'All you've said so far is about church. Is this an issue anywhere else?'*

Think about it this way: who in the scriptures accomplished anything for God by making their own comfort a top priority? In fact, who in any pursuit—business, sports, education, medicine, etc.—was able to accomplish anything powerful while seeking to remain comfortable?

It can't happen. Almost by definition, if we are going to accomplish anything powerful, unusual, or positive, we have to get out of our comfort zone to do it.

Think of the biblical examples. God told Abram, "Leave your native country, your relatives, and your father's family, and go to the land that I will show you" (Genesis 12:1). He had no directions, he had no Google Maps or GPS, and he didn't even have a destination! He simply had a call from the Lord, and he obeyed!

Think of Moses's story.

He was hiding on the backside of the deserts of Midian. He had run away from Egypt, his homeland, after he had killed a man there. (Read Exodus 1–2 if you're unfamiliar with the story.) He knew that he could not go back. There would be *big* trouble there if he did! So as he's tending sheep in the backcountry, isolated and alone, safe and comfortable, he sees a bush that is on fire but does not burn up!

He goes to investigate.

> "This is amazing,' Moses said to himself. "Why isn't that bush burning up? I must go see it."
>
> When the Lord saw Moses coming to take a closer look, God called to him from the middle of the bush, "Moses! Moses!"
>
> "Here I am!" Moses replied.

> "Do not come any closer," the Lord warned. "Take off your sandals, for you are standing on holy ground. I am the God of your father—the God of Abraham, the God of Isaac, and the God of Jacob." When Moses heard this, he covered his face because he was afraid to look at God." (Exodus 3:1–6)

Moses knows this is an incredibly unique experience! This doesn't happen to just anyone! God appearing to a man? Almost unheard of! He must be wondering, *What's going on? Why me? Why here?*

The Lord continues speaking from the bush.

> "I have certainly seen the oppression of my people in Egypt. I have heard their cries of distress because of their harsh slave drivers. Yes, I am aware of their suffering. So I have come down to rescue them from the power of the Egyptians and lead them out of Egypt into their own fertile and spacious land. It is a land flowing with milk and honey—the land where the Canaanites, Hittites, Amorites, Perizzites, Hivites, and Jebusites now live. Look! The cry of the people of Israel has reached me, and I have seen how harshly the Egyptians abuse them." (Exodus 3:7–9)

This is good, Moses might be thinking. *God's going to intervene! He's going to rescue the people back there in Egypt!*

Then the Lord drops the hammer. "Now go, for I am sending you to Pharaoh. You must lead my people Israel out of Egypt" (Exodus 3:10).

Wait. What? Who? *Me?*

God is coming to call *Moses* to lead the people out of Egypt!

He will have to leave his comfort and anonymity and go to the very place he escaped from! This would be decidedly *un*-comfortable!

Usually, the things the Lord asks us to do are! You can't accomplish anything for God by staying comfortable.

It's not only the Old Testament either. Think of just a few examples in the New Testament.

The Holy Spirit calls Phillip to go out into the desert road that runs from Jerusalem to Gaza—about fifty miles. Doesn't tell him why. On that road, he comes across an official from Ethiopia who had been in Jerusalem to worship and was heading back home. That official is reading out loud the book of Isaiah.

The Holy Spirit tells Phillip to walk up to the chariot. When he does, Phillip hears him reading from Isaiah 53 about the suffering servant who would die for the sins of others. There in that precise place, at that precise moment, Philip leads that man to Jesus. When they find water, he gets baptized by Philip. Then Philip is miraculously taken away!

Philip was simply told to go walk on a road—a long, lonely, and at times, dangerous road. He doesn't know why or what he's looking for, but he does it anyway. He *just so happens* to meet the official, who *just so happens* to be reading out loud from Isaiah, and it *just so happens* to be the scriptures that were fulfilled in the person and work of Jesus Christ! This *divine appointment* could not have happened if Philip decided to stay in place and remain "comfortable."

You can't accomplish anything for God by staying comfortable.

In Acts 10, the apostle Peter was called by the Holy Spirit to reach out to a Roman soldier who lived in Caesarea but had basic faith in God. Peter was told to go to his house and even eat food that had previously been off-limits! The Lord was moving Peter out of the comfortable ways of his past and his religious upbringing and instructing him to step out and reach out to the Gentiles—a very *un*-comfortable thing for him to be sure!

There are simply too many examples in the scriptures to cite: Elijah and the ravens, the widow, the prophets of Baal, and rain; David and the giant, Goliath; Jonathan and his armor-bearer against the Philistines; Daniel and his friends standing up to King Nebuchadnezzar, etc. And it wasn't only men! Rahab rescuing the spies from Israel, Deborah leading the people of Israel, Jael killing the leader of the Canaanite army who had attacked Israel, and of course, Mary, the earthly mother of Jesus Christ!

Now *that* was an uncomfortable situation (Luke 2), but you never accomplish anything for God by remaining comfortable!

Actually, the better way to say it is this: God will not accomplish anything in the life of someone who insists on remaining comfortable rather than stepping out and following His will! On the other hand, the Lord's Word says, "The eyes of the Lord search throughout the whole earth seeking to strongly support those whose hearts are fully committed to Him" (2 Chronicles 16:9).

So how about it?

Are you ready to cast aside the idol of comfort, leave behind your insistence on comfort, security, and routine, and step out to follow Him? Are you willing to listen for His voice and follow where He leads—whatever the course? Are you willing to be uncomfortable for His call? Are you willing to risk your safety and security in order to fulfill His call to you?

If so, start to pray that way!

Look for the small ways God might be whispering to you to step out and obey! Listen for God's leading as He ignites within you a fire to follow and honor Him!

I believe that God still calls His people—followers of Jesus Christ—to accomplish big things in His name and for His glory. Most of us simply have not developed ears that hear.

He whispers to us to do something—even something relatively small—and we ignore His whisper.

He may whisper to us to invite a friend to church, He may whisper to send a card to someone, He may whisper to give a financial gift or to buy a lunch for a homeless person on the street.

Many times, we simply write these things off.

We ignore the whispers and the promptings and choose instead to remain comfortable in the life that we've grown used to. But God wants to develop our faith. He wants to teach us how to step out in that faith and listen to Him then to follow and see Him work!

Here's the thing: in most cases, God will not lead us to do anything *great* in life if we refuse to listen and obey the *small* things. The *little acts of obedience* are the training ground for the big things. If we want God to do big things in us, we must first learn to listen and follow through—no matter how uncomfortable it is—in the small things.

I remember once, when the Lord had been teaching me lessons on listening to His prompting, that I was driving on US 131, the highway near my home—just outside of Kalamazoo, Michigan—in the winter. It was a freezing night, and I just wanted to get to my destination and get warm again.

As I was driving south, I saw a man walking on the north side of the divided highway. I didn't think much of it until I drove about another half mile and saw a van on the side of the road, its hood open. I could see a family inside (little kids, mom in the passenger seat—you get the idea).

Immediately I felt the Lord whispering to me, 'Go pick him up and give him a ride.'

I wrestled a little with it. I was in a hurry, he might not have wanted a ride, and someone else might have picked him up. But I knew what I had to do. I went to the next exit, turned around, and went back. I passed his family in the van and saw him still walking. I pulled over just ahead of him and called out, "Want a ride?"

"Yes!" he said, and then he climbed in. He thanked me for stopping; it was so cold out there.

I drove him to the next service station and waited with him as he made arrangements to have them come and tow his van and help him.

I offered a ride back to his family. As a dad myself, I knew that I would be concerned for my family in that situation! He gladly accepted, and I drove him back. As I dropped him off, I assured him, "I just want to tell you I'm a Christian and I'm going to be praying for your family tonight."

He thanked me and got out.

Now I don't know what that meant in the overall scheme of eternity. I don't need to know. What I do know is that I believe that the Holy Spirit of God prompted me to do something and I did it, and I became a little blessing within the midst of a stressful time for that family that night.

That night, I heard the whisper. I overcame my desire for comfort and put obedience to the Lord before my own selfish desires. To be sure, there are other times that I've missed the whispers and missed the opportunity to be used by God. I don't want to do that anymore!

I believe that God is whispering to His children all the time. We often miss it because our own comfortable routine gets in the way.

What would it do to our lives if we started to listen for the whispers and were willing to step out of our comfort zones and started to serve Him?

What would it do to our churches if our seats started to be filled with people who were hearing God's whispers, sensing His promptings, and willing to step out and follow?

What would it do to our culture to have millions of Christians who realize that God *still* does great things and that He does those things through them?

Imagine a group of people, millions strong, who are ready and willing to step out into the adventure of following the Lord's plan!

Now *that* would be an awesome thing!

And it can be!

Are you ready? Are you willing? Are you listening?

Let's go!

CONCLUSION

THE ANSWER!

So, after all of this, what is the solution for America, for the church in America, and for each one of us?

Our country—in general—is quickly moving further and further away from God's influence. We have become increasingly guilty of our own modern form of idolatry.

As a culture, especially over the past six decades, we are more frequently saying no to God.

Materialism, self-centeredness, abortion, gay marriage, drug culture, general immorality, political pandering, religious syncretism, comfort, sexual sin, violence, etc. Every one of these things stand in opposition to the teachings of the Word of God.

Individuals may disagree with the Word of God, and in this country, you have a right to do so. That does not make the Word of God wrong, however, nor does your disagreement result in God's Word changing.

It is true it was never the case that America was *technically* a Christian nation.

Nations can't be Christian any more than any other group can be.

Individuals are Christians, and they may band together to stand for Jesus and His Word, but America is not now, and has never been, a theocracy like Israel was.

Israel was founded by God. He selected Abram and determined to make him "father of a great nation," (Genesis 17). America did not enjoy that status.

Yet America *was* founded on Judeo-Christian principles, and many of the founders were committed Christians who saw this as a country most definitely dedicated to God, lived with the example convinced that, like Israel, this country had a special place in history and a special opportunity to make itself *God's way*.

And as long as we've kept to those principles, we've been the most prosperous, most generous, and most powerful nation in history!

Not a nation without flaws, to be sure. Still, a unique and God-friendly nation.

Unfortunately, over the last six decades, our culture has changed dramatically. We've increasingly turned our backs on God and His Word and sought to become a nation guided by relativism and the desire *not to offend*, rather than a nation that confidently and boldly staked its future on following the Judeo-Christian God—albeit very imperfectly.

If we, as a nation, have declared for over two centuries that we are a nation who wants to be "One Nation, under God" and we say, "In God we trust" but rebel against Him, He will remove His blessing and then *will* send discipline upon us.

How drastic that discipline is depends on *us!*

That pattern is shown throughout the scriptures, and I believe we are seeing that unfold in our country today.

Despite what some politicians say, this world is not safer, our economy is not more stable, and our people are not more optimistic than ever. In fact, I believe it to be just the opposite, and it continues to be so! These things are a bit scary, and they should be!

What is to be our response? We—the church—should lead the way.

And therein lies the problem. As I've stated, the church in America has, in many cases, grown comfortable and lazy. We have adopted our *American idols*.

As the apostle Peter said, it is time for "judgment to begin with the house of God" (1 Peter 4:17), and I believe it is time for the church in America to have another 'come to Jesus' meeting.

Gone are the days when we could sit back and do nothing and hope that our culture—politicians, courts, businesses, and media—would stand up for the *right* thing and make it easy on us. I believe that the days are coming when it will be increasingly difficult to stand up as a Christian and declare our allegiance to Him. Yet that's exactly what we need to do!

Jesus said,

> "You are the salt of the earth. But what good is salt if it has lost its flavor? Can you make it salty again? It will be thrown out and trampled underfoot as worthless.
>
> You are the light of the world—like a city on a hilltop that cannot be hidden. No one lights a lamp and then puts it under a basket. Instead, a lamp is placed on a stand, where it gives light to everyone in the house."
> (Matthew 5:13–15)

The whole point of a lamp is to *give light!* Even in the darkest corners.

Salt, He said, is only good as long as it keeps its saltiness—its ability to contribute "spice" and flavor as well as to be used as a preservative. Otherwise, it's worthless and thrown out.

Has the church in America been acting like "salt" and "light"? Have *you*?

Have you committed yourself to living with Him as Lord of your life, reading, studying, and obeying His Word? Have you committed yourself to standing up for the truths in His Word, regardless of what your culture, family, and friends do? Have you committed yourself to being His ambassador, as Paul calls us, to the extent that we are actively seeking to share the good news about Jesus Christ to family, friends, coworkers, and even strangers, if the Holy Spirit leads?

I hope the answer is *yes*; I fear the answer is, in many ways, *no*.

We are *not* living with this mindset. And that, I believe, is why the church has quietly gone along with its own silencing. We have become content to be left alone, not ruffling any feathers, not offending anyone with the truth.

Like the proverbial frog in the pot, we have apathetically relaxed as the water has been progressively turned up on us, to the point where we're just about cooked!

Is there any hope for us? Any hope for America?

I believe there is!

Look at 2 Chronicles 7. Take a look at verse 14. Just before this verse, God told the people of Israel that 'there may be times that I'm going to discipline you and it's going to get ugly.'

When that happens, he says,

> "If my people who are called by my name will humble themselves and pray and seek my face and turn from their wicked ways, I will hear from heaven and will forgive their sins and restore their land." (2 Chronicles 7:14)

- "If my people who are called by my name ..."

    Not 'America.' Originally this was, of course, directed to the nation of Israel. I believe it is now legitimate to say this could be applied in part to His followers—the church! Christians—You and I!

- "... will humble themselves and pray and seek my face and turn from their wicked ways ..."

Purposeful, passionate, genuine repentance and confession—turning our lives back to Him.

- "Then I will hear from heaven and will forgive their sin and will heal their land."

He will start by restoring *us* as His children, reviving *us*, and then He will move out into our churches, our neighborhoods, our country.

We don't need to worry so much about what's going on *out there*, in the sense of protests, etc. We need to be more concerned about what God wants to do *in here*—the hearts, minds, and behavior of the church in America!

We need to be about *His glory* more than about our rights. We need to bring our own lives—every area of them—into subjection to His will.

Our culture may not understand. In some cases, they may turn against us. After all, anytime anyone calls someone else out, and calls them to live by a higher standard and to change their lives, there is often resistance.

Many times in history, that resistance to God and His Word has been in the form of persecution.

It still is. All over the world, Christians are being persecuted for trying to follow the Lord. While we should resist this and should encourage our leaders to speak up in protest to this, it should not surprise us.

Jesus warned that it would be that way.

> "If the world hates you, remember that it hated me first. The world would love you as one of its own if you belonged to it, but you are no longer part of the world. I chose you to come out of the world, so it hates you. Do you remember what I told you? 'A slave is not greater than the master.' Since they persecuted me, naturally they will persecute you. And if they had listened to me, they would listen to you. They will do all this to you because of me, for they have rejected the one who sent me." (John 15:18–21)

For over two millennia, the church has withstood the persecutions that have arisen and has responded with more boldness, more practical acts of courage and love, and more sharing of the Gospel.

It started in the early days of the church when the persecution began. The church scattered around the world, but they didn't run away and hide; instead, they consistently shared the good news about Jesus everywhere they went!

As a result, the Gospel spread had more impact and inspired people to take bold new steps, such as striking out and seeking to establish a nation dedicated to God, living out the values in His Word, and boldly and consistently following Him.

I believe that's still the best hope for America.

But whatever God's plan for America as a political entity, I *know* that's God's plan for His people—those all over the world who continue to view themselves more as citizens of heaven than as citizens of this earth.

As we—you and I who are believers and followers of Jesus Christ—unashamedly declare our allegiance to Him, follow His Word, and seek to live all of life by His example, our hope is that we will have increasing influence on our family, friends, and neighbors.

We need to embrace honest evaluation, authentic repentance, complete confession, and a renewed commitment to *true worship of the true God!*

We must remember that God created us, that He loves us, and that His ways are for His glory and our good! Following His will in all these things—not the world's plans—is the best prescription for the best life.

Casting down our idols and worshipping Him with our love, our words, our actions, and our lifestyles is now, and always has been, our best and greatest hope.

May the Lord make it so!

CPSIA information can be obtained
at www.ICGtesting.com
Printed in the USA
LVHW100150220722
724144LV00005B/144

9 781664 252011